REGATHERING POWER

Regathering Power

John Michael Talbot
with
Dan O'Neill

c. 1988

SERVANT BOOKS
Ann Arbor, Michigan

Published by Servant Books
P.O. Box 8617
Ann Arbor, Michigan 48107

Printed in the United States of America
ISBN 0-89283-610-5
88 89 90 91 92 10 9 8 7 6 5 4 3 2 1

Read:
pages 20-21

Contents

Abbreviations in Text of Documents of Vatican II / vii
Preface / ix
Introduction / xi

1. Powers of Darkness: The Bad News / 1
2. Truth Power: The Good News / 19
3. Spirit Power: A Pentecost Church / 35
4. Empowerment: Getting There / 45
5. Music Power: Worship, Thanksgiving
   and Praise / 61
6. Staying Power: Community and Personal
   Discipline / 77
7. Program Power: Evangelization / 101

Abbreviations in Text of Documents of Vatican II

AA—*Apostolicam Actuositatem*, Decree on the Apostolate of the Laity of the Second Vatican Council

EN—*Evangelii Nuntiandi*, Evangelization in the Modern World, Paul VI, 8 December, 1975

GS—*Gaudium et Spes*, The Pastoral Constitution on the Church in the Modern World of the Second Vatican Council

Preface

IN 1983 DAN O'NEILL WROTE my authorized biography, *Troubadour for the Lord,* to the public acclaim of both critics and readers. This successful team was formed because of my own time limitations and Dan's literary talents. Also, we share a common spirituality as brothers on similar journeys in Christ from evangelical Protestant to the Catholic faith. This shared experience gives both of us a truly interdenominational outlook. *Troubadour* was the beginning of a close friendship and working relationship which fostered many joint world relief and development projects with Mercy Corps International. We also founded Franciscan Mercy Corps in 1987.

It is with much joy that Dan and I again team up for this, our second book together. Dan's writing abilities and his spirituality are obviously maturing with the passing of the years. For those familiar with my other books, you will, no doubt, discern some difference in writing style. Some will say it is better. Some will say it is worse—not pure "JMT." I can only assure the reader that Dan and I have spent many hours preparing the text of this present book. We have pored over my past books, as well as transcripts of my many seminars and lectures. Furthermore, we have enjoyed countless hours just brainstorming and praying together as good friends in Christ. No doubt, the style is an integration of Dan's and mine. But I also have no doubt that Dan has accurately captured the essence of my message and communicated it skillfully. This present book would simply not be possible without his expert and careful participation.

In 1978 I privately published a paper entitled, "The Regathering." This work explained to my evangelical brothers and sisters the "whys" of my conversion to the Catholic faith. In it I also presented an outline for unity between Catholics and evangelicals based on mutual understanding and concrete action.

This book, *Regathering Power,* is a more public work. In it I use the same principles for unity as in the first private paper. But instead of centering on doctrines, I zero in on issues and the power of the Holy Spirit. As the Second Vatican Council says, "If in moral matters there are many Christians who do not always understand the gospel in the same way as Catholics, and do not admit the same solutions for the more difficult problems of modern society, nevertheless they share our desire to cling to Christ's word as the source of Christian virtue.... Hence, the ecumenical dialogue could start with discussions concerning the application of the gospel to moral questions." I also emphasize spiritual phenomena like the charismatic renewal, basic Christian community, and personal disciplines of asceticism and prayer.

I encourage readers to enjoy this book. It includes an overview of many topics I have treated in the past with the addition of much new material. I believe the subject matter is on the cutting edge of current issues facing the church in the modern world. As with my first effort with Dan, I pray that this will pave the way to many more follow-up works which will bear much fruit in building God's kingdom. As with my first "Regathering," I pray it will help bring unity to the fragmented Christian churches so that we might meet the awesome issues that challenge the very existence of life in our modern world.

—John Michael Talbot

Introduction

WE ARE LIVING IN THE NEW POST-CHRISTIAN ERA. Ours is an age which has cast off the ancient Judeo-Christian faith and the values that have been part of that faith. According to contemporary philosophers and ideologues, the traditional church has lost its relevance. These modern prophets claim that only the dawn of a "new age" can bring humankind to its fullest expression and ultimate destiny.

What about the Christian message of the apostles? Is the church really an archaic, outmoded anachronism in these closing years of the 20th century? Or could the ancient call of faith be more timely now than ever before? If the church is to address today's most critical challenges, it must go forth in authority, conviction, and power. The same power from on high which anointed the fledgling church in Jerusalem on Pentecost must be central to our corporate Christian agenda for modern times.

The stakes are higher now than ever before in the history of the world. The threat of nuclear war, new resistant viruses such as AIDS, genetic engineering, frightening ecological disorders, the scandal of global hunger, and the holocaust of the unborn threaten the very existence of modern society. As St. Paul says, "The wages of sin is death but the gift of God is eternal life through Jesus Christ our Lord." These immense challenges are calling us to a radical, redemptive proclamation of the gospel of Jesus Christ. Unquestionably the task is almost overwhelming. We are called to continue evangelizing a needy world and this requires tremendous power. Sufficient for the task is the very power which created the universe and resides within each believer. With this realization the mandate of world evangelization can be engaged confidently, forcefully, and successfully.

Let me make it clear at the outset that I am writing out of my own spiritual tradition, which is both Roman Catholic and charismatic. I have a deep love and respect for both of these traditions, and it is my hope to share with readers about the real insights that stem from them. Even so, I do not expect all of my Protestant brothers and sisters to agree with or embrace everything in the book. I am not trying to outline the ultimate plan for unity, but only to offer my personal perspective for living together as Christians in a world which seems to be very rapidly falling apart. As such, I hope that both Catholics and Protestants will find help in this book, and that every reader will be called to a more radical commitment to live only and fully for Jesus, the pioneer and perfecter of our faith.

This book is a call to daily conversion to Christ—and to the spiritual empowerment needed to confront and conquer a world which hangs in the balance between the forces of darkness and the Light of the world. Specifically, I hope to present Christ's answers to the awesome challenges which confront the church and threaten the very existence of the world and to share these answers in light of the Scriptures, Franciscan sources, and the teaching of Vatican II, which I believe can be of benefit to both Catholic and Protestant Christians. I do this in an attitude of sharing rather than trying to proselytize my Protestant friends.

As the Catholic church has so clearly proclaimed, "Today, the human race is passing through a new stage of its history . . . a true social and cultural transformation. . . . This transformation has brought serious difficulties in its wake." The answer? "The church believes that Christ, who died and was raised up for all (2 Cor 5:15), can through his Spirit offer man the light and the strength to measure up to his supreme destiny. . . . The church also maintains that beneath all changes there are many realities which do not change and which have their ultimate foundation in Christ, who is the same yesterday

Hebrews 13:8

and today, yes and forever (Heb 13:8)" (GS, no. 10).

More than in any other time in history Christians must stand together as a unified people to face these awesome challenges. They are too great to face alone, or even as fragmented denominations, fellowships, or groups. This is a time that demands unity. When I speak of unity in this context, I do not mean that all denominations will join together to create one large structural church. I mean the kind of unity in which Catholics and Protestants acknowledge one another as brothers and sisters in Christ. I mean the kind of unity in which we can work side by side to resist the forces of darkness that threaten to engulf our world.

This book suggests ways for all Christians to respond to these issues as a united people. Granted, there are still many differences within the body of those who call themselves Christians. We cannot, at this time, clear up all of our differences on a doctrinal or a sacramental level. But we can identify the critical issues of our time and agree on some appropriate moral responses. Because Christianity is not essentially a religion of "law" but of a personal love relationship with Jesus Christ, I will also consider the work of the Holy Spirit who empowers us to respond and will discuss ways to persevere in this radical call from Christ.

We can use as our pattern for unity the dispersion and regathering of the Jews. In the beginning, God established a leadership, lifestyle and worship for the people of Israel. He gave them a law and a land to dwell in. But because of the sins of the leaders, the Lord scattered the people and demonstrated that he was their ultimate shepherd.

When God issued the call through the prophets to be regathered from the dispersion, the people were called to return to Israel, to once again be united.

The dispersion and regathering of the Jewish people is a pattern for what I see among Christians today. Because of sin, we have been divided and scattered, weakened in our ability to be a people together. Today, more than ever, I believe God is calling for a "regathering" of his people, spread over the face of the earth. This means that Catholic and Protestant leaders must ultimately learn to work together. The worship and experience of Protestants and Catholics must be harmoniously integrated, while respecting the uniqueness of each. The wealth of revelation that God has so freely distributed to all his people must be integrated into an ever-developing understanding of Christian truth.

I realize, of course, that this regathering is a massive undertaking, but we must begin somewhere. Someone must lift his voice to begin to proclaim God's call. That is what this work is all about. It is only a beginning. As was said in the preface, we cannot expect to enter into full unity all at once. Responding to the call of unity, however, begins with the consideration of some urgent moral issues of our time, and I propose a unified Christian effort in meeting these challenges with both Protestant and Catholic sources.

Because God has chosen to pour out his Spirit in a charismatic renewal which has swept across Catholic and Protestant barriers, I will also spend several chapters examining the pentecostal dimension of every believer's life. One chapter will also investigate the phenomenon of intentional Christian community, which, like the charismatic renewal, has moved across church barriers. Finally, I will look at personal disciplines applicable to all Christians.

Protestants and Catholics have a great deal to learn from one another. Just as the Jews had to be regathered before the first coming of Jesus, it may be that Catholics and Protestants now will be regathered in unity to prepare for the second coming of Christ.

ONE

Powers of Darkness:
The Bad News

HOW WELL I REMEMBER THE EXCITEMENT and awe we Americans felt when NASA's Apollo lunar missions placed men on the surface of the moon. As a young person, I was proud to be living in an era, and in a country, which overcame enormous technological barriers in order to fulfill our wildest space travel dreams! In particular, I recall one of the Apollo astronauts describing the beauty of the planet earth, from the moon. With feet firmly planted in the gray dust of the desolate lunar landing site, he gazed through the inky darkness of space toward a luminescent, blue-green sphere; so beautiful, so fragile, suspended like a delicate jewel in the cosmos.

No wonder so many Apollo mission astronauts have experienced profound inner changes as they gazed upon God's wondrous creation from their remote point of observation. Indeed, it seems a miracle that human beings have been able to unshackle the bonds of earthly gravity in order to project our presence into space. But how is it, I wondered, that the very creatures which have forged deeply into space through their startling technological advances, still inhabit a planet which is troubled—even tortured—by the most basic and life-threatening of curses?

More than five billion people now crowd the planet earth. As the multitudes continue to multiply, we find ourselves facing greater challenges to our survival than ever. Ironically, in an era when our economic power and technological brilliance could bless the world in countless ways, we find ourselves haunted by lethal threats, most of which we have caused. How can it be that while a deep interplanetary probe sends back volumes of electronic data, complete with stunning photographs of unexplored worlds, countless children die of starvation? "The modern world shows itself at once powerful and weak, capable of the noblest deeds and the foulest. Before it lies the path to freedom or to slavery, to progress or retreat, to brotherhood or hatred. Moreover, man is becoming aware that it is his responsibility to guide aright the forces which he has unleashed and which can enslave him or minister to him" (GS, no. 9).

The problems we face today as fellow citizens on the earth are too great to number. However, certain of these problems are so critical that they must be mentioned to bring into focus the darkness which stalks us in the latter part of the 20th century. If we are to gather together in the power of Christ to overcome the power of darkness, it is important that we understand the extent of the darkness that threatens us.

Materialism and Poverty

As our Western society continues to upgrade its standard of living, a large proportion of the world's population suffers from malnutrition and related illnesses. Not long ago I had an opportunity to travel to the Central American country of Honduras with Mercy Corps International, an ecumenical Christian relief and development agency which I have supported for several years. I was appalled to find that on America's doorstep, rural village peasants earn an average of less than $100 a year. Malnutrition, illness, and infant mortality are at shocking levels only a two-hour plane ride from

Miami. Since then I have traveled to other Third World nations. The story of hunger and poverty is the tale of most of this world, yet I live in a country that enjoys greater comfort than ever known before. United Nations experts now say that 40,000 people, mostly children, die each day from malnutrition, yet most agree that the West has within its technological capacity the ability to feed the entire world.

> Never has the human race enjoyed such an abundance of wealth, resources, and economic power. Yet a huge proportion of the world's citizens is still tormented by hunger and poverty, while countless numbers suffer from total illiteracy. Never before today has man been so keenly aware of freedom, yet at the same time, new forms of social and psychological slavery make their appearance. . . . For political, social, economic, racial and ideological disputes still continue bitterly, and with them the peril of a war which could reduce everything to ashes. . . . Some nations with a majority of citizens who are counted as Christians have an abundance of this world's goods, while others are deprived of the necessities of life and are tormented with hunger, disease, and every kind of misery. This situation must not be allowed to continue to the scandal of humanity. . . . (GS, no. 4)

War

Directly related to the scandal of global poverty is the curse of war. When people lack basic human rights they grow frustrated. When they grow frustrated enough, they rise up in revolt. As St. James says, "Where do the conflicts and disputes among you originate? Is it not your inner cravings that make war within your members? What you desire you do not obtain, and so you resort to murder." But this does not justify the materialistic oppressor. James continues, "As for you, you rich, weep and wail over your impending misery. . . . Here, crying aloud are the wages you withheld from the farm hands who harvested your fields. The cries of the harvesters have reached the ears of the Lord of Hosts."

As Isaiah the prophet says, "Make justice your aim. Redress the wronged, hear the orphan's plea, defend the widow." Or again, "Woe to those who enact unjust statutes and who write oppressive decrees, depriving the needy of judgment and robbing my people's poor of their rights." It is only when we fulfill the prophet's command of justice toward the poor that we will fulfill his prophecy, "They shall beat their swords into plowshares and their spears into pruning hooks. One nation shall not raise the sword against another, nor shall they train for war again."

Certainly not all wars are the result of oppressed people rising up in revolt. All too often the greed for power and domination among the leaders of the world give rise to conflict after conflict. Wars in the Third World flare up like brush fires around our planet, each threatening to pull the superpowers into dangerous new levels of confrontation. How well I recall a peaceful, sunny day on one of my visits to the Holy Land. I had gone out to the Mount of Temptation in the desert to pray and contemplate when suddenly the quiet was shattered by the roar of Israeli war planes (made in the U.S.A.) maneuvering in the skies above. But it wasn't only my peace which was being shattered. International peace in the Middle East has been virtually unknown for a generation. It is one of the many nuclear fuses which threaten the human family with a total, global holocaust.

Nuclear War

We have reached a time in the history of the earth when we are capable of destroying ourselves through the use of vast arsenals of holocaust weapons which do not distinguish between combatants and the civilian masses. We now possess the means to snuff out all life on the planet within a matter of days. And it can happen by accident. "The horror and perversity of war are immensely magnified by the multiplication of scientific weapons. For acts of war involving these weapons can inflict massive and indiscriminate destruction far exceeding the bounds of a legitimate defense. . . . These considerations compel us to undertake an evaluation of war with an entirely new attitude. . . . Any act of war aimed indiscriminately at the destruction of entire cities or extensive areas with their populations is a crime against God and man himself. It merits unequivocal and unhesitating condemnation" (GS, no. 80).

The following quote also comes from the same document: "While extravagant sums are being spent for the furnishing of ever new weapons, an adequate remedy cannot be produced for the multiple miseries afflicting the whole modern world. Disagreements between nations are not really and radically healed. On the contrary other parts of the world are infected with them. . . . Therefore, it must be said again: the arms race is an utterly treacherous trap for humanity and one which injures the poor to an intolerable degree" (GS, no. 81).

War and Peace

"In our generation when men continue to be afflicted by acute hardships and anxieties arising from ongoing wars or the threat of them, the whole human family has reached an hour of supreme crisis in its advance toward maturity" (GS, no. 77). Yet, "Peace is not merely the absence of war. . . . Peace results from that harmony built into human society by its Divine Founder and actualized by men as they thirst after greater justice. . . . Peace is never attained once and for all, but must be built up ceaselessly . . . since the human will is unsteady and wounded by sin. . . . Peace cannot be obtained on earth unless personal values are safeguarded and men freely and trustingly share with one another the riches of their inner spirits and their talents. . . . Insofar as men are sinful, the threat of war hangs over them, and hang over them it will until the return of Christ. But to the extent that men vanquish sin by a union of love, they will vanquish violence as well . . ." (GS, no. 78).

Chemical Dependency

In our attempts to find escape, relief, recreation, and anesthesia from pain and guilt, we have turned to widespread substance abuse. So voracious is the self-destructive appetite for illegal drugs in this nation that concerted military effort or police action cannot prevent the multitudinous rivers of cocaine, heroin, and marijuana from flowing to ever expanding markets from abroad. Incredibly, at a time when American farmers are going out of business in large numbers, it has been said that marijuana has become America's leading cash crop. Alcoholism also continues to enslave and destroy millions of lives, directly through addiction, indirectly through relationships. Twenty-five thousand people a year die on our nation's highways from drunk driving—an incredible toll!

In the 1981 document, "I Have Done My Part, May Christ Teach You Yours," written on the 800th anniversary of the birth of St. Francis, the Franciscans have recognized these problems and some underlying concerns:

> . . . the widespread callous disregard for human needs and rights so evident in the plight of economic and political refugees; of barracks dwellers; of drug addicts; of handicapped; of elderly people discarded like used-up consumer goods—or worse, as a danger to society; of the ever-increasing number of people beset by all types of diseases, notwithstanding the much vaunted progress in the area of health care; of the mentally ill, detained in alarming numbers in psychiatric facilities (or worse yet, left to roam the streets without shelter or care). All of this constitutes a

fearful indictment of the human sensibility of today's world—even of civilization itself with all its alleged progress.

This document points out the more primary problem of human sensitivity and rights, and its devastating "domino effect" which brings down many other moral structures and virtues.

Sex and AIDS

The sexual revolution of the 60s and 70s, in which it was hoped we could free ourselves from unnecessarily stringent social norms in favor of a new freedom, has boomeranged back upon us in the form of increased family breakdown, estrangement, illness, and death. We were not freed. We have become enslaved. Sexual union, which was designed by God for marital intimacy and the transmission of life has, ironically, caused enslavement, division, sickness, and now, through the AIDS epidemic, death on a scale unimaginable only a few years ago.

How well I remember Ray. After a glorious conversion to Christ, he turned from a gay lifestyle. He visited our prayer community and was eager to grow spiritually. But, tragically, he had already been infected with the deadly AIDS virus. Months later he approached me at a New York concert, looking thin and wasted. This thirty-year-old man looked seventy. We embraced and prayed together. Now he is gone. His illness was painful and protracted—his suffering beyond imagination. AIDS will soon touch all of us in different ways. We are all paying a horrific price, even now. While it is important to compassionately and lovingly care for the AIDS victim, it is also urgent that we recognize the spread of this disease as a consequence (except among those who have innocently contracted the virus through transfusions or other means) of moral decisions made by those who have not complied with church teaching on sexual behavior. In short, "hate the sin, love the sinner."

The Catholic church has spoken very clearly on the issue of sex. The document, "Declaration On Certain Questions Concerning Sexual Ethics" (Sacred Congregation for the Doctrine of the Faith, December 1975) says, "The church cannot remain indifferent to this confusion of minds and relaxation of morals. It is a question, in fact, of a matter which is of utmost importance both for the personal lives of Christians and for the social life of our time." Many people accept Jesus' or Paul's teachings on sexuality as only particular applications of the general law of love in the cultural settings of that time. This means that the truth they proclaim, in particular about sexuality, is only relative. Many would say, therefore, that in certain settings, premarital or extramarital sex may be wrong, but in other settings it may be quite acceptable. We must uncompromisingly reaffirm that all genital sex acts must take place within the context of marriage. "Today there are many who vindicate the right to sexual union before marriage. ... This opinion is contrary to Christian doctrine, which states that every genital act must be within the framework of marriage." The sex act must involve "the finality of the sexual act," which is composed of "mutual self-giving and human procreation in the context of love."

Abortion

The war against the unborn continues unabated. Millions are slaughtered in the womb annually by those who would rather not be inconvenienced by caring for a new life and by those who profit handsomely through the clinical factories of fetal death. Cardinal Bernard Law, shortly after his installation as Archbishop of Boston, had these words to say about abortion: "It is the primordial darkness of our time; this is the cloud that shrouds the conscience of our world. Having made our peace with the death of the most innocent among us, it is small wonder that we are so ineffective in dealing with hunger, with injustice, with the threat of nuclear war."

Ethics

In recent months we have seen moral crises hit major political figures, business executives, and television evangelists. These well-publicized scandals have revolved primarily around sex, money, and power and seem to indicate a progressive breakdown in the moral fiber of our society. Integrity in the church and in the marketplace is an increasingly rare commodity.

Jesus had strong words to say about the concept of law: "Do not imagine that I have come to abolish the Law or the Prophets. I have come not to abolish but to complete them. I tell you solemnly, 'til heaven and earth disappear, not one dot, not one little stroke shall disappear from the Law until its purpose is achieved. Therefore, the man who infringes even one of the least of these commandments and teaches others to do the same will be considered the least in the kingdom of heaven; but the man who keeps them and teaches them will be considered great in the kingdom of heaven. For I tell you, if your virtue goes not deeper than that of the scribes and the Pharisees, you will never get into the kingdom of heaven" (Mt 5:17-20). Paul writes in Romans that "the Law is sacred, and what it commands is sacred, just and good" (Rom 7:12). Paul continues, saying that the law is provided out of love. Moral laws are timeless and cannot be eroded because the Lawgiver is changeless: "Jesus Christ is the same today as he was yesterday and as he will be forever" (Heb 13:8).

Ecological Disaster

Each week it seems we hear through the news media of a new area which has been contaminated by toxic waste or dangerous chemicals. In many places, streams, lakes, and the earth beneath us, once beautiful and pristine, now ooze the stuff of death and illness because the very technological advances which should bless us have, through greed and deceit, become a curse. At the same time that deserts, particularly in Africa, continue to swallow productive farmland at a frightening pace, scientists point out that the protective ozone layer around the earth is eroding. Without it, we are exposed to harmful rays of the sun which may one day strike down millions with withering disease and which may irreparably damage the delicate ecosphere from which we draw life.

The following quote is powerful and relevant to our current situation and comes from the Franciscan document, "I Have Done My Part, May Christ Teach You Yours":

Contemporary awareness of the ecological problems gives us a strikingly appropriate context in which to proclaim to our brothers and sisters the intimate relationship that should exist between God, human beings and the cosmos. This harmony, broken by sin and restored by Christ (Romans 11:15, Colossians 1:10, II Corinthians 5:19), was entrusted once again to human beings by the risen Lord; but our response has, over the centuries, been only too clear; we have abused our trust and allowed to disintegrate what God has created good and reconciled in His Son made man (Ephesians 1:10, Colossians 1:20).

During the past few decades, in fact, we have shown less respect than ever for nature, as a spectacular masterpiece of God's goodness and wisdom. We thought we had the right to do as we pleased, without ever taking into account the complex interrelationships that characterize nature's rich and tremendous harmony. Precisely because we have so wantonly violated the sacred relationship between ourselves and nature—a bond intricately woven into our very nature as human beings—we are today the impoverished spectators of all sorts of unforeseen and ever more threatening consequences. Indiscriminate destruction of plant and animal life, the ongoing depletion of our water supply, the atmospheric pollution that has by now become nearly universal, and the resulting spread of incurable diseases are but a few indications of the alarming situation in which we find ourselves because of the way we have upset the balance of nature.

Another powerful statement was made by an assembly of American bishops on November 30, 1971 in the document, "Justice in the World":

Men are beginning to grasp a new and more radical dimension of unity; for they perceive that their resources, as well as the precious treasures of air and water—without which there cannot be life—and the small delicate biosphere of the whole complex of all life on earth, are not infinite, but on the contrary must be saved and preserved as a unique patrimony belonging to all mankind. Such is the demand for resources and energy by the richer nations, whether capitalist or socialist, and such are the effects of dumping them in the atmosphere and the sea that irreparable damage would be done to the essential elements of life on earth, such as air and water, that their high rate of consumption and pollution, which are constantly on the increase, were extended to the whole of humankind.

The New Age Movement

No wonder that in the midst of such international crises we see a renewed search for answers, for meaning, for transcendent values with which to cope. I believe this is why we see a "New Age Movement." The gurus of enlightenment are now telling us that we are on the threshold of an entirely new era during which time we will find fulfillment, direction, and rescue from our many disasters. It is said that channeling, spiritual guides, occult mysticism, international harmonic convergence, and other manifestations will usher in a new messianic age of peace and well-being never before experienced.

This is simply a lie. The amazing thing is that it is being swallowed by so many well-educated individuals who should know better but who, in their need, are captivated by a relativistic gospel which promises self-gratification on a spiritual scale. Some Christian leaders and Christian organizations have even been drawn into this deception.

Indeed, the conditions of our day are a grim reminder of Christ's apocalyptic statements in Matthew, chapter 24:

> And Jesus answered them, "Take care that no one deceives you; because many will come using my name and saying 'I am the Christ,' and they will deceive many. You will hear of wars and rumors of wars; do not be alarmed, for this is something that must happen, but the end will not be yet. For nation will fight against nation, and kingdom against kingdom. There will be famines and earthquakes here and there. And this is only the beginning of the birth pangs.

All this has been brought home to me personally in my own travels. I have witnessed a coup attempt in the Philippines, an earthquake in Los Angeles, a hurricane in London, fighting in the Persian Gulf, and a global stock market crash. And this has all taken place over a brief period of weeks! In addition, the prophetic word, from both Protestant and Catholic sources, indicates a time of coming chastisement for the nations and peoples of the West.

Recently I have seen almost every ministry I know and work with go through major change. These changes have threatened their very existence. Likewise, I have seen families and communities endure intense trials and reorganization. Those who held on to Jesus made it through the storm. Those who did not, perished in the raging waters of confusion, frustration, and despair.

While walking the grounds of the Alverna Retreat Center in Indianapolis, God gave me a word: "The earth is shifting." I did not hear that the earth was being destroyed. It was only "shifting." This meant that God was putting things in their proper place. But the shift involved change. Like an earthquake, the earth's geological plates must move. Only when they stop moving or "jam" do they then give way in the sudden jolt we call an earthquake. So it is with spiritual life. When we "jam" the natural movement of God, then there will be a "quake" in our life as God gets things moving again.

Ironically, the "new age" heresy is not new in the church. In the 12th and 13th centuries the prophecies of Joachim of Fiore also predicted a new age. In his prophecies, the dispensation of the Father was the Old Testament, the dispensation of the Son was the New Testament and the apostolic church, and the dispensation of the Spirit was yet to come in which a whole new ecclesiology and theology would be established before the second coming of Christ. This apocalyptic message appealed to the whole of Europe during the 13th century and was embraced by many serious Christians, especially the eccentric spiritualist branch of the early Franciscan movement. Of course, it totally overlooked that the age of the Spirit had already begun with the outpouring of the Spirit on the first Christians of Pentecost.

Today too, the "new age" message appeals to those trying to regain the pristine purity of the first Christians, while breaking free from the legalistic yoke of Christian traditionalism. No doubt, it appeals to the emotions as they witness the seemingly new outpouring of the Spirit on those of all denominations. But today, as in the past, this theology is in conflict with the already existent reality of Pentecost. The new age is nothing more than the old paganism, rearing its head once more.

The new age, therefore, presents major problems. Since it is "new," it has no consistent links with any recognized religious leadership, nor any one single leader or unified group of leaders. Consequently, any truths about faith and morality are up for grabs. Truth varies from guru to guru, from devotee to devotee. This relativistic approach to faith has given birth to a highly inconsistent, or individualistic morality. In many cases this translates to gross immorality when viewed from a Christian perspective. Ironically, this is precisely the new age movement's appeal to highly immoral and individualistic cultures such as our own.

Undoubtedly there is a real and authentic need which millions are sensing, but the answer does not lie in a new age. Yes, there is development. But there is no new age. Jesus is the fulfillment of a new and final age. There is no "new" new covenant. There is no new Bible. There is no new church. Don't be deceived. Christ is our foundation and the rock of our salvation. He is the alpha and the omega, the beginning and the end. "The church has always had the duty of scrutinizing the signs of the times and of interpreting them in the light of the gospel. Thus, in language intelligible to each generation, she can respond" (GS, no. 4).

Has Christianity Failed?

If Jesus Christ is the answer and the church is Christ's body on earth today, why do we not see multitudes opting for an authentic gospel instead of cop-outs, diversions, escapism, false religions, and misguided new age philosophies? Why is it that the church's witness does not go forth with more authority and power? Part of the reason is because today's church is debilitated by internal divisions which confuse the unchurched and make it difficult for them to recognize Christ's presence among his people.

We lack unity. Not only has the body of Christ been fragmented through schisms and controversy, but even individual denominations find themselves locked in tremendous turmoil and conflict. The state of the Christian people is a scandal in the eyes of the world and contradicts Christ's teaching that we must be one as he and the Father are one.

Christians share the fault for the widespread atheism that

atheism

exists in the West. "Believers themselves frequently bear some responsibility for this situation. For, taken as a whole, atheism is not a spontaneous development but stems from a variety of causes, including a critical reaction against religious beliefs, and in some cases against the Christian religion in particular. Hence believers have more than a little to do with the birth of atheism. To the extent that they neglect their own training in the faith, or teach erroneous doctrine, or are deficient in their religious, moral, or social life, they must be said to conceal rather than reveal the authentic face of God and religion" (GS, no. 19).

Frequently Christianity seems to lack power if not objective truth. Some time ago I spoke with a Christian counselor who had been dealing with many people grappling with severe problems. He knew that his answers and his insights were technically correct but, nonetheless, he experienced many failures—far too many. While he had a technical understanding of the problem, he was unable to communicate the answers with force and conviction. He was not empowered.

The church often lacks boldness or a convincing witness. To be sure, there are individual figures who command our respect because of their radical fulfillment of gospel values, such as Mother Teresa and Billy Graham. However, mainstream Christianity is judged by many to be weak and anemic. We are in the midst of a kind of malaise; a pervasive lukewarm stew of confusion, timidity, and slumber.

Whatever happened to the explosive renewal of the late 60s and early 70s? It was an era when Catholics and Protestants alike moved out in power and conviction preaching the gospel, healing the sick, and bolstering their efforts with disciplined prayer, fasting, and study. The "Jesus People" presented a street-level, radical witness to Christ which shook entire cities and landed the movement a cover shot on *Life* Magazine. Out of this sweeping renewal Christian publishing and Christian music burst forth with powerful, uncompromising messages centered around total conversion to Christ and commitment to ongoing spiritual development. During this time many Christian ministries to the poor were raised up to give the gift of love and life to millions throughout the world.

But now what do we see? In a recent letter, Billy Ray Hearn, president of Sparrow Records, penned the sobering message which follows:

> I am very concerned about the Christian music business. There is obviously a serious problem. Sales are very soft and there does not seem to be any one answer. After a lot of prayer and discussion, I believe God is definitely speaking to all of us in the body of Christ. Historically, music has been the handmaiden of God accompanying great spiritual revivals or movements. In today's church, however, there seems to be no great spiritual awakening or enthusiasm.

It is no real wonder that there is an industry-wide crisis in the Christian music business. Christian music exploded in the wake of renewal—as a consequence of revival. When the renewal began to fade, so did Christian music.

Music and lyrics which attempt to mimic the world will never inspire. Christian musicians who have attempted to cross over into secular success have watered down their message and are becoming unpalatable to Christians searching for Jesus-centered songs of praise and worship. And, technically, these performers can't achieve secular production standards. Of course, we understand that the Christian message must be marketed, whether it is record albums or Bibles. But when marketing dictates spirituality and art, the dollar becomes an idol—a false god. Those Christian artists who maintain a clear call to Christ and an uncompromising message of faith, however, continue to be in demand even though they may not produce big budget albums.

The same may be said about the Christian publishing business. After a recent Christian Booksellers Association convention, the executive vice president of a prominent East

Coast publishing company said flatly, "It's all over." I asked what he meant. He stated simply that the Christian publishing world is sliding from big-time sales into relative obscurity as interest has waned in the manuscripts which are currently being published.

International Christian ministries are also hurting. Many of those which have geared their efforts toward the world's poor have been damaged by the scandal of unethical television evangelists as well as "compassion fatigue." There seems no consistent depth of commitment to the poor beyond emotional crises such as Ethiopia. Even though we could continue to give the gift of life out of our tremendous material blessings, it seems we just don't care. We have done our part, we say, and the world continues to die, spiritually and physically. We are in sorry shape—we are failing.

But wait. Do not despair. Jesus Christ established his church in the promise of power—a power which promotes unity, boldness of witness, signs, wonders, love, compassion, and the persistent strength to proclaim Christ's name throughout the world. The power which created the very universe literally resides in each one of us who call ourselves Christians. "Greater is he who is within us than he who is in the world!" The Holy Spirit empowers and renews, bringing us to repentance and salvation in a conversion process which must be engaged daily.

I believe we are entering a period of judgment. I don't think God is going to destroy us, but he is going to correct us. There may not be a nuclear holocaust or a Marxist takeover. I just believe we will lose our creative edge. We may slip into a syndrome much like post-Christian Europe, where there are a lot of churches, but where there is very little living faith. This is a death worse than destruction. It is a living death. No doubt, we are materialistic, so God will take away much of our wealth and give it to others. No doubt, we are sexually promiscuous, so God will make it a fearful and dangerous thing to engage in sex outside of heterosexual marriage. The list goes on. Yes, we will face trial, but it is of our own making. If we simply repent and turn back to God and his design for this world, we will again prosper. Until then we will experience judgment.

It is my conviction that judgment must and, in fact, has begun in the house of the Lord. Once cleansed, renewed, we will capture the same explosive power that characterized the charismatic movement of the 60s and 70s. The challenges I mentioned earlier are not to be taken lightly. They threaten life on our planet—nothing could be more serious than that. However, the hope that resides within us in the person of the Holy Spirit can empower us to meet these challenges head on.

I remember the now legendary story from charismatic renewal circles of the mid-70s. Bob Mumford, an almost larger than life leader in the movement stopped suddenly, in the midst of a sobering message to 50,000 people assembled at Arrowhead Stadium in Kansas City in the summer of 1977 and raised a riotous response with a divinely inspired victorious exclamation. "I took a look at the back of the Bible," he shouted, "and I found out that in the end, Jesus wins!" The crowd roared and erupted into Spirit-led, spontaneous worship for more than ten minutes. This moment has been known among charismatics as "the great Holy Ghost breakdown" (*Charisma*, August 1987).

The thought of Christ's victory must continue to encourage us, giving wings to our hearts and spirits. But beware—we are called to do our part, to convert, to grow, to follow, to radically and completely serve Christ through the power and presence of the Holy Spirit in our lives and in Christian community.

Don't grow faint! Lift up your hearts! Trust in the Lord, commit your ways to him and be renewed. Yes, there is plenty of bad news—more than enough to go around. But there is also the eternal gospel of Jesus Christ. And that is Good News!

TWO

Truth Power:
The Good News

J ESUS SAYS, "YOU WILL KNOW THE TRUTH and the truth will set you free." Before the crucifixion Pilate asked, "What is the truth?" And all the classic philosophers—from the earliest Ionians to Socrates, Plato, and Aristotle—all sought after a universal truth, one that would never change, one that could always be relied upon by all peoples for all time.

Jesus said, "I am the way, the truth, and the life." And the book of Hebrews says, "Jesus Christ is the same yesterday, today and forever."

Jesus quoted Isaiah regarding his mission on earth, "The Spirit of the Lord is upon me; therefore, he has anointed me. He has sent me to bring glad tidings [good news] to the poor, to proclaim liberty to captives, recovery of sight to the blind and release to the prisoners, to announce a year of favor from the Lord." And to his disciples he said, "If you live according to my teaching, you are truly my disciples; then you will know the truth and the truth will set you free."

The Bible

But how do we discover the truth that Jesus Christ taught? Oh yes, it is easy to say "just read the Bible." But why do we believe in the reports of Jesus in the Bible?

One reason for believing is because of the witness of the Holy Spirit within us. As Jesus said, "I will ask the Father and He will give you another Paraclete—to be with you always: the Spirit of Truth." Or again, "I have much more to tell you, but you cannot bear it now. When he comes, however, being the Spirit of Truth, he will guide you to all truth." As Paul says, "The Spirit himself gives witness with our spirit that we are children of God."

So the Spirit bears witness with our spirit that the words of and about Jesus in the Bible are true. This kind of witness is beyond proof or disproof. As Paul said, "The spiritual man can appraise everything, though he himself can be appraised by no one."

Even so, this approach can create problems. One person claims the Spirit told him to interpret the Scripture one way. Another person claims the authority of the Spirit for an interpretation that is entirely different. Both claim only to be relying on the literal interpretation of the inspired word of God. This has been the cause of divisions in the church since the beginning, especially in the past 400 years which have seen the church torn into a thousand pieces.

The problem arises because we look at the Scriptures themselves backward. Instead of understanding that the Bible came to us through the early history of the church, we assume that it somehow dropped out of the sky from God and just appeared in the hands of the church. But this is not how we got the Bible.

If we examine the history of the Scriptures we will discover a fundamental truth: the Scriptures came out of the life of the Christian people. If we want to understand a debatable passage of Scripture today, we should go back to the church from which the Scriptures came, to see how the early Christians interpreted the passage. If they had one particular or most common approach we can apply that ancient interpretation to our situation today in a developed way, and maintain a unity with the early church. Likewise, if we deny the authority of the church from which the Scriptures came, we destroy the authority of the Scriptures themselves. Let us now look at some specific characteristics of the truth of the New Testament.

Jesus, Incarnation of Truth

Truth of N.T.

First of all, the truth of the New Testament is not just a cold collection of written facts. The center of the Old Testament was the law. But good and true as the law might be, it is not complete.

Paul says the full truth is "a letter written not with ink but by the Spirit of the living God, not on tablets of stone but on tablets of flesh in the heart." As is said in the beginning of the Gospel according to St. John, "In the beginning was the Word—and the Word was God—the Word became flesh and made his dwelling among us, and we have seen his glory." And as John says at the beginning of his first letter, "This is what we proclaim to you: what was from the beginning, what we have heard, what we have seen with our eyes, what we have looked upon and our hands have touched—we speak of the word of life."

The truth of the New Testament, therefore, is not just objective writings. It is the incarnate person of Jesus himself. Our truth is not lifeless and cold, like tablets of stone or a book printed by a machine in a factory. Our truth is warm and personal. He took on flesh and blood. He laughed and cried, took on our joys and sorrows. He understands us, not only because he created us, but because he has lived among us as one of us. This is a truth I can understand. This is a teaching that comes from experience.

As Hebrews says, "For we do not have a high priest who is unable to sympathize with our weakness, but one who was tempted in every way that we are, yet never sinned. So let us confidently approach the throne of grace to receive mercy." Or, "Son though he was, he learned obedience from what he suffered; and when perfected, he became the source of eternal salvation for all who obey him." Or again, "Indeed, it was fitting that when bringing many sons to glory God, for whom and through whom all things exist, should make their leader in the work of salvation perfect through suffering. He who consecrates and those who are consecrated have one and the same Father. Therefore he is not ashamed to call them brothers."

So the truth—the man Jesus—came into this world. He gathered followers, or disciples, and from them chose the twelve as apostles. So there is a succession of this living truth through living persons—Spirit to spirit, Heart to heart, and Flesh to flesh—from Person to person.

The Apostles

We know that Jesus "called the Twelve together and gave them power and authority," and "He sent them forth to proclaim the reign of God." We know that he taught them his own teaching during his ministry: "If you live according to my teaching, you are truly my disciples." And that he taught them from existing Scripture after his resurrection, "Beginning, then, with Moses and all the prophets, he interpreted for them every passage of scripture which referred to him." We know that before his ascension he gave them the "great commission" in these words, "Full authority has been given to me both in heaven and on earth; go, therefore, and make disciples of all the nations. Baptize them in the name of the Father, and of the Son, and of the Holy Spirit. Teach them to carry out everything I have commanded you."

So Jesus gave the apostles a "teaching authority" based on their personal time with him and his personal choice of them. He even gave them the authority to discern the truth of a person's conversion and the right or wrong of their faith and moral choices. "Whatever you declare bound on earth shall be held bound in heaven, and whatever you declare loosed on earth shall be held loosed in heaven." Many Christians believe he gave this same power to Peter, adding in a special way, "I, for my part declare to you, you are 'Rock' and on this rock I will build my church, and the jaws of death shall not prevail against it. I will entrust to you the keys of the kingdom of heaven."

He also empowered them with the Holy Spirit in a special way, for leadership: "Then he breathed on them and said, 'Receive the Holy Spirit. If you forgive men's sins, they are forgiven them; and if you hold them bound, they are held bound.'" Of course, they, like all believers, were empowered by the Spirit at Pentecost. "You will receive power when the Holy Spirit comes down on you; then you are to be my witnesses."

So the Twelve, chosen by Jesus himself, under the special leadership of Peter, were sent forth to proclaim the truth and establish the church. They had been with Jesus from the beginning. They had personally heard his teachings and been instructed by him concerning the correct interpretation of Scripture. Furthermore, they had been empowered for this special ministry by the Spirit of truth through Christ.

It is because of this reality that we see the first church in Jerusalem devoting themselves "to the apostles' instruction" rather than going off on their own to try to decipher the "real" message of Jesus. It is because of this that we see Peter's role of leadership in the early church.

It was Paul who said, "The gospel I proclaim to you is no mere human invention. I did not receive it from any man, nor was I schooled in it. It came by revelation from Jesus Christ." And Paul who "directly withstood [Peter], because he was clearly in the wrong," ultimately submitted to the teaching authority of the original apostles, in particular, Peter, James, and John. "I went prompted by a revelation, and laid out for their scrutiny the gospel as I present it to the Gentiles, to make sure the course I was pursuing, or had pursued, was not useless." It was this confirmed apostolic authority in Paul which could cause him to say without hesitation, "If anyone preaches a gospel to you other than the one you received, let a curse be upon him!" It was also this authority which enabled him to judge the incestuous man in Corinth, and restore him to communion with the church after a time.

The Apostles' Successors

We know that as the apostles went forth throughout the world, they themselves attracted followers and disciples as they formed the church. From their disciples they appointed leaders as their successors in a particular church, to insure that the truth of the gospel be passed on and preserved in the very way it was received.

As the Acts of the Apostles says of this process, "In each church they installed presbyters and, with prayer and fasting, commended them to the Lord in whom they had put their trust." Of Paul himself, with Barnabas, it says, "While they were engaged in the liturgy of the Lord and were fasting, the Holy Spirit spoke to them: 'Set apart Barnabas and Saul for me to do the work for which I have called them.' Then, after they had fasted and prayed, they imposed hands on them and sent them off." And as Paul says to Titus, "My purpose in leaving you in Crete was that you might accomplish what I had left undone, especially the appointment of presbyters in every town."

In this way the truth of Jesus Christ was imparted to the church and the world. Thus, this transmitted truth had living authority through the life of the Spirit-led church. It had apostolic authority through discernible succession from the apostles themselves. Therefore, it ultimately carried the authority of Christ himself, for Christ had sent both the apostles and the Spirit to guide his church according to the love and truth of the gospel.

Scripture

It was from this apostolic church that the Scriptures came. As the church spread to other cultures it became appropriate, and even necessary, to write the story of Jesus so that it might be published and read by many more people. What made more sense than to have the remaining apostles or their close companions, write these accounts? Likewise, as the established churches began to encounter conflict from within and without, it became necessary for those with apostolic authority to write letters to help clear up problems. This is how both the gospels and the letters of the New Testament were written. In addition, a secret tract was written during the Roman persecution to encourage Christians and to instruct them about the "latter days." This is what we call "The Revelation," the "Apocalypse," or "the unveiling." All of these were written during the first century of the church's existence, and represent the most ancient expressions of the faith of the apostles.

But it was many centuries before we had a "Bible," "biblios," or a "collection of books." Many gospels were written. Many letters bore the names of apostles. Some of those conflicted with one another. Some were simply redundant and irrelevant. Which should be included in the "Bible"?

This decision was left to the successors to the apostles, the bishops. Some bishops came up with lists that partially agree with the content of our present Bible in the 3rd and 4th centuries. There was more widespread agreement by the 5th century. But there was still disagreement by a few as late as the 9th century! Only with the Council of Trent did the Catholic church authoritatively establish the canon of the Catholic Bible.

Development

The canonization of Scripture brings out the whole principle of "development." As John's Gospel says of Christ, "I have much more to tell you, but you cannot bear it now. When the Spirit comes, however, being the Spirit of truth, he will guide you to all truth." This means that as the church meets particular circumstances, obstacles, and questions in history, she will have to bring the timeless universal message of the gospel to the world in a developed way, so as to meet the particular challenges of a given time. It was just such a process that brought us the Bible itself.

Common Roots

It is with this understanding that Christians everywhere, both Protestant and Catholic, are coming to a more credible understanding of the truth of Jesus Christ as brought to us through the Bible. Catholics and Protestants alike are growing closer together as we all rediscover our unity with the early church through the power of the Spirit of Truth at work in our individual lives.

It is from this living, balanced, and developed perspective that we can now look at the problems that face our modern world in the light and challenge of the gospel of Christ. Without the flexibility of the concept of development, the gospel becomes archaic and antiquated, stuck in the past, unable to speak to the present or build toward the future. Without the authority to proclaim some truths as universal and timeless, the church becomes paralyzed and irrelevant—like a "reed blown in the wind" of human opinion and constantly changing circumstances. Both approaches lead to frustration and eventual despair.

Let us look now at a few of the problems mentioned in Chapter One.

Materialism and Poverty

We need to do more than simply identify the bad news. We need to bring forth an answer based on the gospel of Jesus Christ. Jesus says very clearly, "Sell what you have and give alms," or "Whenever you give a lunch or dinner, do not invite your friends or brothers or relatives or wealthy neighbors.... Invite beggars and the crippled, the lame and the blind." As to the trap of materialism, he says, "Avoid greed in all its forms. ... Do not lay up for yourselves an earthly treasure.... None of you can be my disciple if he does not renounce all his possessions." Or, "You cannot serve God and money."

These teachings prompted the first church in Jerusalem to "sell their property and goods, dividing everything on the basis of each one's need." Thus they could say, "Nor was there anyone needy among them."

As the church spread throughout the world, a more lenient approach was adopted. "The relief of others ought not to impoverish you; there should be a certain equality," says Paul to the Corinthians. This is permissive, but it is still radical. Equality between rich and poor in the Christian community is a pretty high ideal!

Is there equality today? Is there equality between the church of the First and Third Worlds? Is there equality between the old inner-city parish and the new one in the suburbs? Is there even equality between the rich and the poor of a local parish? I am afraid the answer is no. We do not even live up to the minimum requirements of the church of the New Testament, much less the example of Jesus Christ.

Last year I went shopping with a friend in Berryville, Arkansas. I noticed that my companion was purchasing the very best of every product on the shelves—the most expensive foods in the most attractively designed packages. I commented on the prices and pointed out that through group purchases and careful generic brand shopping one can save a significant amount of money. As a Franciscan, I pointed out that the funds saved by altering our shopping practices could be given to the poor. The principle is simply this: if many people make small sacrifices, an enormous amount of good can be done in sharing for the poor. This is something we can all do, regardless of our specific calling or vocation.

The Catholic church teaches very specifically regarding wealth: "Man should regard his lawful possessions not merely as his own but also as common property in the sense that they should accrue to the benefit of not only himself but of others." Or, "The right to have a share of earthly goods sufficient for oneself and one's family belongs to everyone. The Fathers and Doctors of the Church held this view, teaching that men are obliged to come to the relief of the poor" (GS, no. 69).

As to distribution of wealth, the Catholic church says, "The distribution of goods should be directed toward providing employment and sufficient income for the people of today and of the future" (GS, no. 70). It is a basic human right to have the necessities of life: food, clothing, shelter, medical treatment, a good job, the freedom to raise a family and other basic needs. It is the responsibility of a just government to permit these rights.

Catholics do not, however, support a total communism. "Private ownership . . . should be regarded as an extension of human freedom." It is viewed as a basic human right. "The right to private control, however, is not opposed to the right inherent in various forms of public ownership. By its very nature, private property has a social quality. If this social quality is overlooked, property often becomes an occasion of greed and of serious disturbances" (GS, no. 71).

In short, we are neither to support the forced atheistic communism of Marxist-type governments, nor the usual disproportionate wealth and greed of Western capitalism. We are to steer a middle ground between these two extremes. This third way is badly needed in trouble spots throughout the world. This middle ground is balanced and true, yet it is radical because it is rooted in the gospel of Jesus Christ.

War and Peace

Jesus strikes at the heart of war by teaching the doctrine of nonresistance. "You have heard the commandment 'an eye for an eye, a tooth for a tooth.' But what I say to you is: offer no resistance to injury. When a person strikes you on the right cheek, turn and offer him the other. If anyone wants to go to law over your shirt, hand him your coat as well." This gives feet to his beatitude, "Blessed are the peacemakers."

St. Paul says, "If possible, live peaceably with everyone. Beloved, do not avenge yourselves; leave that to God's wrath. 'If your enemy is hungry, feed him; if he is thirsty, give him something to drink; by doing this you will heap burning coals upon his head.' Do not be conquered by evil but conquer evil with good."

Based on these and other similar Scriptures the Catholic church teaches, "Peace is not merely the absence of war. Peace results from that harmony built into human society by its divine Founder, and actualized by men as they thirst after ever greater justice" (GS, no. 78). As to nonresistance, "We cannot fail to praise those who renounce the use of violence in the vindication of their rights."

After roundly condemning the arms race, this document offers ways and means toward international peace: "It is our clear duty, then, to strain every muscle as we work for the time when all war can be completely outlawed by international consent. Peace must be born of mutual trust between nations rather than imposed on them through fear of weapons" (GS, no. 82).

Leaders are encouraged to "extend their thoughts and their spirit beyond the confines of their own nation, that they put aside national selfishness and ambition to dominate other nations" (GS, no. 82).

The cause of war? Very similar to the words of St. James: "If peace is to be established, the primary requisite is to eradicate the causes of dissension between men. Wars thrive on these, especially on injustice. Many of these causes stem from excessive economic inequalities" (GS, no. 83). These words, undoubtedly, sting the conscience of Americans who, though we are a minority of the world's population, still control over 75% of the world's wealth.

The church then goes on to encourage international organizations to facilitate dialogue and mutual support between nations. Specifically, "In the field of social life this means food, health, education and employment" (GS, no. 84). Again, "there must be an abolition of excessive desire for profit, nationalistic pretensions, the lust for political domination, militaristic thinking and intrigues designed to spread and impose ideologies" (GS, no. 85).

Lest, however, we find these hopes too idealistic: "Insofar as men are sinful, the threat of war hangs over them, and hang over them it will until the return of Christ" (GS, no. 78). As Jesus says, " 'Peace' is my farewell to you, my peace is my gift to you; I do not give it to you as the world gives peace. Do not be distressed or fearful."

As one Franciscan Rule says, "As they announce peace with their lips, let them be careful to have it even more within their own hearts. No one should be roused to wrath or insult on their account, rather all should be moved to peace, good will, and mercy because of their gentleness. The sisters and brothers are called to heal the wounded, to bind up those who are bruised, and to reclaim the erring." That this peace is primarily internal and spiritual, the rule continues, "Wherever they are, they should recall that they have given themselves up completely and handed themselves over totally to Our Lord Jesus Christ. Therefore, they should be prepared to expose themselves to every enemy, visible and invisible, for love of Him because the Lord says: 'Blessed are they who suffer persecution for the sake of injustice, theirs is the kingdom of heaven.'" If we could follow the admonition of this rule, we would do well.

So we are called to work for peace in this world. We are given some very tangible ways, means, and goals. But we are also warned to keep our eyes on the eternal dimension of the gospel of Jesus Christ rather than getting sidetracked into the political and temporal arenas. Jesus is our lasting peace.

Ecology

The awareness of the problem of ecology is a rather new one. It is an abuse we are all guilty of, and a sin whose consequences we all share.

Even though this is a rather new problem, there are Scriptures which give us some answers and some hope. Jesus, of course, based many of his parables on examples from nature. He referred freely to the lilies of the field, the birds of the air, the seeds of the sower and the wheat and the tares. He saw all the realities of creation as reflecting the glory of God. As Paul says, "Since the creation of the world, invisible realities, God's eternal power and divinity, have become visible, recognized through the things he has made."

The Scriptures also promise that a Christian understanding of stewardship will free, rather than enslave, creation. Again, Paul says, "The whole created world awaits the revelation of the sons of God. Creation was made subject to futility, not of its own accord but by him who subjected it; yet not without hope, because the world itself will be freed from its slavery to corruption and share in the glorious freedom of the children of God." Paul says of the ministry of Christ, "In him everything in heaven and on earth was created, things visible and invisible, whether thrones or dominations, principalities or power; all were created through him and for him. He is before all else that is. In him everything continues in being—it pleased God to make absolute fullness reside in him and by means of him, to reconcile everything in his person, both on earth and in the heavens, making peace through the blood of his cross." If Jesus gave his life to help reconcile creation to God, shouldn't we adopt this attitude as well?

The Franciscan document, "I Have Done My Part, May Christ Teach You Yours," encourages us in this mission:

Contemporary awareness of the ecological problem gives us a strikingly appropriate context to proclaim to our brothers and sisters the intimate relationship that should exist between God, human beings, and the cosmos. This harmony, broken by sin and restored in Christ was entrusted once again to human beings by the risen Lord. We Franciscans do have a fully appropriate and adequate solution to this humanly insoluble predicament. If we can but make our own the attitude of Francis, the mystic and troubadour of nature, we can enlighten our brothers and sisters, educate them, lead them to appreciate and embrace a correct approach to creation. In his Canticle of Brother Sun, the Saint of Assisi has celebrated all the works of creation: the sun, the moon and the stars of heaven; the wind, the earth with its flowers, plants, and fruits—Francis had an intuitive sense of all creatures' sacred character, and he paid them due respect both because of their intrinsic value and because of their availability to human beings. Prophets of doom notwithstanding, we can in our day reverse current trends. We can protect our environment. And we have no better means at our disposal than a renewed sensitivity to nature's true meaning and value—a sensitivity flowing from Christian vision, so well understood and put into practice by Saint Francis."

Sexual Immorality, Abortion, AIDS

The problem of sexual promiscuity is as old as the human race. Happiness and fulfillment are promised, and all that is found is emptiness, pain, and death. As James so aptly says, "The tug and lure of his own passion tempt every man. Once passion has conceived, it gives birth to sin, and when sin reaches maturity it begets death." And Paul also says, "Just as formerly you enslaved your bodies to impurity and licentiousness for their degradation, make them now servants of justice for their sanctification. When you were slaves of sin, you had freedom from justice. What benefit did you enjoy? Things you are now ashamed of, all of them tending toward death. . . . The wages of sin is death."

Jesus speaks to the origin of sexual promiscuity when he says, "You have heard the commandment, 'You shall not commit adultery.' What I say to you is: anyone who looks at a woman has already committed adultery with her in his thoughts." As Scripture says, "The root of all conduct is the mind." Paul also speaks of the thought process. But instead of saying what not to think, he recommends some positive mental discipline: "Your thoughts should be wholly directed to all that is true, all that deserves respect, all that is honest, pure, admirable, decent, virtuous, or worthy of praise."

Jesus also recommends some healthy principles of asceticism here. "If your right eye is your trouble, gouge it out and throw it away! Better to lose part of your body than to have it all cast into Gehenna [hell]." This could apply to both actions and tempting circumstances or to thoughts as well.

Paul speaks of a mental asceticism in this process. "You must lay aside your former way of life and the old self which deteriorates through illusion and desire, and acquire a fresh, spiritual way of thinking. You must put on that new man created in God's image, whose justice and holiness are born of truth."

This involves bringing your very thoughts to the cross—of changing your thought processes by crucifying the old process and replacing it with something better. As Paul continues, "Bring every thought into captivity." And on the principle of the cross and resurrection as it pertains to sexual immorality, "It is obvious what proceeds from the flesh: lewd conduct, impurity, licentiousness, drunkenness, orgies and the like. I warn you, as I have warned you before: those who do such things will not inherit the kingdom of God! In contrast, the fruit of the Spirit is love, joy, peace . . . and chastity. Against such there is no law! Those who belong to Christ Jesus have crucified their flesh with its passions and desires. Since we live by the Spirit, let us follow the Spirit's lead."

As we have seen from the last chapter, Catholic teaching on the subject of sexuality is quite clear. All genital expressions of sexuality must involve "mutual self giving and human procreation in the context of true love . . . within the framework of marriage" (GS, no. 51). This rules out masturbation, where there is no mutual self giving, homosexuality, where there is no procreation, and all premarital and extramarital relations.

The more basic concept of respect for human life is the thread which ties all the teachings of the Scripture and the church together. It is respect for your own life, the life of your spouse, and the life of the yet unborn, which cause all these teachings on sexuality to make sense. It is respect even for the very process of life.

"For God, the Lord of life, has conferred on men the surpassing ministry of safeguarding life—therefore from the moment of its conception life must be guarded with greatest care while abortion and infanticide are unspeakable crimes" (GS, no. 51). This is why the Catholic church also teaches that to unnaturally impede the process of life is to distort God-given procreation.

If we can grasp this principle of life we can solve most of the problems of our world. Life reflects the Giver of life, and the abuse of life abuses God. To impede life is to attempt to impede God. This more primary truth solves all the problems mentioned in Chapter One: poverty, war, crime, sexual immorality, and the resulting spread of diseases such as AIDS, abortion, chemical dependencies, and even the present ecological disorder.

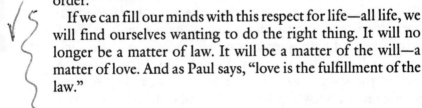

If we can fill our minds with this respect for life—all life, we will find ourselves wanting to do the right thing. It will no longer be a matter of law. It will be a matter of the will—a matter of love. And as Paul says, "love is the fulfillment of the law."

THREE

Spirit Power:
A Pentecost Church

THE FIRST CHAPTER LISTED SOME of the awesome challenges facing our modern world. The second chapter outlined a way to find answers to these challenges. The answers are invaluable, but they are not enough. Jesus says, "You will know the truth and the truth will set you free." But Paul says, "No one will be justified in God's sight through observance of the law; the law does nothing but point out what is sinful." Even Paul sometimes did what he hated and so hated what he did. It is good to know what the objective problems are that face us. It is also good to know some of the answers from divine law. But without the empowerment of the Spirit, we are doomed to constantly fail in fulfilling the very law we know to be true.

Consider the experience of the apostles and the disciples of the early church. They lived with Jesus. They saw him heal the sick, raise the dead, and feed the multitudes. They heard his teachings firsthand. They saw Jesus remain true to his own teaching of love, even to the point of death. They experienced the almost unimaginable excitement of the resurrection. They were personally tutored by Christ in the teachings of the Old Testament which actually referred to his own messianic advent. They finally saw him ascend to the Father in glory. But even with all this objective truth, they needed something more.

Jesus told them, "Remain here in the city until you are clothed with power from on high." Or again, "You will receive power when the Holy Spirit comes down on you; then you are to be my witnesses in Jerusalem, throughout Judea and Samaria, yes, even to the ends of the earth." It was only with the empowerment of the Spirit that even the truth of Jesus could be fully life-giving. Remember what Jesus said of the work of the Spirit, "When he comes, however, being the Spirit of truth, he will guide you to all truth."

So truth is not enough. We must personally know the Author of truth through the power of the Holy Spirit in our own lives. As Bonaventure says, "No matter how well we plan our spiritual progress, nothing comes of it unless divine assistance intervenes. And divine assistance is there for those who seek it humbly and devoutly." Jesus said, "Ask and you shall receive."

It is not enough simply to know what is wrong. We must be empowered in the knowledge of what is right. Then we will not have time to do the wrong! As an old saying has it, "If you spend your time doing the do's, you won't have time to do the don'ts."

If we simply join together to do what Christ has asked Christians of all denominations and faiths to do, we would find ourselves too occupied with *doing* the gospel to fight over the less important interpretations of the gospel. This doesn't mean our differences would disappear. It just means they would be in sharper perspective. This is actually what could transpire when Christians of all denominations open up to the power of the Spirit and join together to fight the evils of this generation with a truth from on high.

Radicals for Christ

We are called to be radicals for Christ. But we are not to be fanatics. A radical is "rooted," like a "radish." A fanatic takes a particular external dimension of true radicalism and emphasizes it to the point of absurdity. We must be deeply rooted in Christ and the gospel. He is "the vine, we are the branches." He then transforms everything about us, from our spirituality to our sexuality, from our prayer life to our economics and politics. This is how we will become spiritual and social revolutionaries for Christ. In Christ we will turn the world upside down, and in so doing, right side up!

To be a radical for Christ is a daily process. It is not a one-time decision. As Jesus says, "Take up your cross daily." For me this means starting each day with these words: "Praise to you, Lord Jesus Christ, King of endless glory." I say this prayer as a discipline, and it starts each day on the right foot. I then go on to practice the prayer and meditation practiced by my particular community. Regular spiritual discipline helps keep me alive. It stirs up my spiritual life and channels my emotions to support my life in Christ rather than to detract from it. It keeps me on course as a Catholic Christian. It keeps me on fire as a Franciscan charismatic. Spiritual discipline keeps me radical for Christ.

It should by now be quite apparent that the message of this book is directed to those who call themselves Christians. It is my assumption that the reader is at least basically familiar with the gospel—with the good news of Jesus Christ. You may be a true Christian zealot; you may be a new babe in Christ; perhaps you are confused and angry with God; or maybe you just feel weak and are looking for true power in your life. You may be spiritually depressed or you may have fallen away from the practice of the Christian faith, but you are open, searching, and hoping. To all, I would simply say this: commit yourself totally this day to Christ. Please don't procrastinate. As Scripture says, "Today is the day of salvation." As Jesus said, "Behold, I stand at the door and knock." The psalmist also wrote, "If today you hear his voice, harden not your heart."

Confess your sins to him and embrace Jesus your Savior each hour of each day. Let your first waking thoughts center upon Christ and upon your true identity as one of his beloved children. The Holy Spirit has called you in the past, is calling you now, and will continue to call you to Christ. But a word of caution! Your commitment should not be viewed as a one-time act or a single step. Conversion must be regarded as a series of steps—walking, as it were, with increasing balance and control. Jesus exhorted his followers to take up their crosses daily. This means salvation is a lifelong process. It requires God's ongoing grace, but it also requires our daily personal response.

Now, in the words of a popular devotional song, it is time for those who have found Christ to "pass it on." Once you have become a member of God's great family through Christ Jesus, you'll want to share with others the blessing of eternal life and friendship with God. But you cannot truly share what you do not actually possess. You cannot bring revolution if you have not first been revolutionized. You cannot evangelize unless you have first been evangelized. You cannot bring justice unless you have first been justified. You cannot bring forth peace in a desperate, violent world unless you first know inner peace. You cannot give the gift of salvation unless you have been saved.

Revolutionaries for Christ

We must be revolutionaries for Christ and, in keeping with a revolutionary strategy, we must propagate the revolution with power and unflinching personal conviction. I have said it many times in interviews, letters, books, in concerts and even in records: as I travel throughout this nation I clearly sense a thirst, a hunger, and a readiness for renewal. Millions of Christians in America are looking for a revolution—a spiritual street-level revolution of love which I call "the gentle revolution."

This Christian revolution must be based on more than mere excitement. The initial excitement we have with anything in life is temporal and will inevitably diminish. The gentle revolution must be undergirded and sustained with enthusiasm. Enthusiasm might be defined as educated excitement which is tempered by sound teaching and evidenced by measurable ongoing growth.

It is the Holy Spirit who draws us to Christ. It is this same Spirit who convicts us and reproves us of our sin. The Spirit of God will revolutionize us and empower us for a very specific task. Before we discuss the concept of Spirit power in more depth, I want to remind you of the task which awaits us. It is the mandate of the church and, indeed, the vocation of each individual Christian: to evangelize the world.

Consider the following quotations (italics mine) from one of the best documents I have ever read on the *"revolutionary"* mission of the church, "On Evangelization in the Modern World," December 8, 1975, Pope Paul VI:

> Jesus himself, the Revelation of God, was the *first and principle herald of the gospel.* This he was until the end, until the consummation in the sacrifice of his human life. . . . For this same Jesus who declared: 'I must preach the good news of the Kingdom of God' is he of whom John the evangelist affirmed that he had come and was destined to die in order 'to *gather into one* the children of God who are scattered abroad.' In this way he accomplishes his revelation, completing and confirming it by the complete manifestation of himself which he achieves *by his words and his works, by signs and miracles, and above all by his death and resurrection and by the sending of the Spirit of Truth.*
>
> Those who sincerely accept the good news, by virtue of it and the faith which it generates, are united in the name of Jesus so that they may together seek the Kingdom, build it up and implement it in their own lives.
>
> We wish to affirm once more that the *essential mission of the church* is to evangelize all men. It is a task and mission which the great and fundamental changes of contemporary society make all the more urgent. Evangelization is the special grace

and vocation of the church. It is *her essential function.* The church exists . . . to preach and teach the Word of God so that through her the gift of grace may be given to us, *sinners may be reconciled to God.* . . . (EN, nos. 7, 12-14)

In the same way that Jesus came to reveal the Father and to reconcile us to the Father, we as God's people are called to reveal Jesus and his great salvation and consequent reconciliation. This document goes on to say that the church cannot truly evangelize unless she herself is constantly renewed:

Accordingly the *church begins her work of evangelization by evangelizing herself.* As a community sharing a common faith and a common hope which she proclaims and communicates to others by her life, and sharing likewise a common fraternal love, it is essential that she should constantly hear the truths in which she believes, the grounds on which her hope is based and the new command of mutual love. As the people of God which has been placed in the world and is often tempted by its idols, she needs to hear constantly the *proclamation of 'the mighty works of God'* by which she has been converted to the Lord so that *she may hear his call anew and be confirmed in unity.* To put the matter briefly, if the church is to preserve the freshness, the ardour and the strength of her own work of preaching the gospel she must herself be continuously evangelized. (EN, no. 15)

In other words, the church, and every one of us as individual members, must continue to be evangelized by constant conversion and renewal so that we might evangelize the world with credibility—and power!

Empowered for the Task

If we are to preach the gospel to every nation and tongue, we must be *empowered* for the task. Again, read these quotes carefully—quotes from Pope Paul VI who, judging by his words, was a true evangelical of monumental proportions, powerfully led by the Holy Spirit:

> In fact, it was only *after the coming of the Holy Spirit on the day of Pentecost* that the apostles set out to all parts of the earth to undertake the great work of evangelization entrusted to the church. Peter explained in their mission to the people as a fulfillment of the prophecy of Joel when he said: 'I will pour out my spirit on all flesh. . . .' Paul is *filled with the Holy Spirit* before undertaking his apostolic mission. Similarly Stephen is full of the Holy Spirit when he is chosen as a deacon and later achieves martyrdom. . . . The Spirit, who caused Peter, Paul, and the twelve to speak, inspiring the words they should say, descends, likewise 'on those who hear the word of God.'
>
> All heralds of the gospel . . . [should] *pray unceasingly to the divine Spirit* with faith and ardour and to submit themselves prudently to his guidance as the principal author of their plans, of their initiatives and their work in the field of evangelization. (EN, no. 75)

I think these words are enormously compelling, inspiring and relevant. Whether Catholic, Orthodox, evangelical, fundamentalist, or mainline Protestant, the call is clear: commit your life to Christ and be a true believer; preach this gospel of love and evangelize the world for Christ; carry out your evangelistic mandate in the power and inspiration of the Holy Spirit.

Time and again, the Catholic church has called us to evangelization in this age. There have been encyclicals on this subject and there have been many programs. It is Christ who will renew his people. He has been doing this through Catholic programs such as RENEW, Marriage Encounter, Cursillo, the charismatic renewal, and other well-known efforts. Protestants have also initiated revitalization programs in witnessing, church growth, Bible studies, leadership training, and other areas. I remember one particular parish I visited which included a large proportion of wealthy people. The pastor sent me a list of over thirty programs which were attempted over ten years. "John," he lamented, "none of them have worked. You know what we did? We finally determined that programs don't renew the church—only Jesus will renew the church. Without him, none of our best-laid plans are going to make a shred of difference." This particular church declared a moratorium on services. They decided to shut everything down except their Sunday liturgy. They put a headline in their church paper that their church was dead and released a statement to their local newspaper that their parish was dead and Jesus was going to have to resurrect it.

I went to that parish to share with the people and to find out what they were thinking. This was a parish which was truly interested in Jesus. After one particular service, we got together in a very small room which was packed with about 300 people. After some moments of silence, one person spoke up and said, "John, we want to be disciples of Jesus Christ. What do we do? We've had enough of programs—we just want to be disciples! We want to get radical. What do we do with our imperfections? What about the poor?" Another spoke up, "What about our cultural restrictions which don't seem to give us permission to really get excited about God?"

This really scared me. Here was a group of highly expectant and searching people, staring at me, seeking direction. I had to be honest. I told them that we can't truly evangelize until we have been evangelized ourselves. We can't save the world or the church unless we have individually allowed Jesus to evangelize our souls. We simply cannot give what we do not have. This is why in many of our churches, in spite of endless renewal programs, nothing seems to happen. We need total, personal conversion. Never before has there been such need for Christians to be radical for Christ and to stand united in their faith.

Unless we are interiorly rooted in Christ through the power of the Spirit, our external works cannot really be radical. They will be fanatical. They will not be effective. So be radical. Then will your soul be renewed. Your life will bear much fruit, allowing you to feed the hungry world with Jesus, the Bread of Life.

FOUR

Empowerment: Getting There

ALL CHRISTIANS ARE CALLED to be Pentecostals. Pentecost is the birthday of the church! Are we "Pentecostal"? We should be! To many, of course, the word "pentecostal" represents a red flag—a load of negative connotations in which we picture the likes of Elmer Gantry, the sawdust trail, holy roller tent meetings, circus-like church revivals, and other images caricaturized by Hollywood or the news media. Let's not give the word "Pentecostal" up quite so easily. Let's take another look.

The Acts of the Apostles says, "When the day of Pentecost came it found them gathered in one place." The account is quite clear. The infant church, in the midst of a mighty, rushing wind, experienced tongues of fire and the miracle of supernatural languages, complete with other signs and wonders, and received enormous Holy Spirit power. It was a power so great that the church exploded into being with many thousands of conversions in a short span of time. So spectacular were these events that within one generation the gospel had spread throughout the entire known world of the Roman Empire. This was not a one-time infusion of high octane fuel, but rather, an empowering by the Holy Spirit that was meant to be renewed throughout the entire church and throughout all the ages. Indeed, we are a Pentecost people, and we must never forget this rich inheritance as we recall our beginnings and regather our vision and power to meet the challenge of our modern world. Just how do we tap into this dynamic power of the Holy Spirit? We know that the Spirit of God takes up residence in each believer. As Paul said, "If anyone does not have the Spirit of Christ, he does not belong to Christ." Clearly, according to Paul, the Spirit of God dwells within us. And the Spirit is offered to many of us through Baptism and Confirmation. But there is more. We must actively and intentionally reach out to receive the gift that has been offered, and we must do so daily. We must actively and consciously make a decision for Jesus, each day, to follow in his steps.

Do We Want the Gift?

But how can we receive the gift of the Spirit? We need only ask! Jesus said, "Ask and you shall receive; seek and you shall find; knock and it shall be opened to you. . . . If you, with all your sins, know how to give your children good things, how much more will the heavenly Father give the Holy Spirit to those who ask him?"

Do all Christians have the Holy Spirit? In one sense the answer is yes. As Paul wrote, "No one can say 'Jesus is Lord,' except in the Holy Spirit." We have all been offered the Spirit in word and sacrament, and it has had an effect on our life . . . whether or not we know it. But in another way the answer is no. As Paul asked the Ephesians, "Did you receive the Holy Spirit when you became believers?" They answered: "We have not so much as heard that there is a Holy Spirit."

So it is with many Christians. We only passively enter into the Holy Spirit's action in our life. But God desires that this relationship with all the persons of the Trinity be not just passive, but active. As we enter into one, we learn more of the other two. Conversely a habitual, passive relationship with any one of the persons of the Trinity weakens our relationship with the other two and our ability to live the Christian life.

Sometimes we do not really know God as a loving Father. Sometimes we don't personally know Jesus as something more than a saving name. More frequently today, many of us do not really have a personal and unquestionable experience of the power of the Holy Spirit.

As you prepare to enter into new dimensions of power through the Holy Spirit, you must be aware that God does not reward those who casually seek him. Rather, he reveals himself and shares his gifts with those who diligently, seriously, and consistently seek his face. Jesus said, "I know your deeds; I know you are neither hot nor cold. How I wish you were one or the other—hot or cold! But because you are lukewarm, neither hot nor cold, I will spew you out of my mouth."

The promise is really quite simple: the Holy Spirit is yours as a Christian and is available in a new and powerful way if you will simply ask in faith and with a clean heart. But you must really want the gift. Paul said, "Set your heart on spiritual gifts."

Stirring Up the Gift

I'll never forget my own special moment (remember, we are each unique individuals, and we may have vastly differing experiences of the Holy Spirit's empowering). I was sitting quietly on an airplane, looking out the window. I gazed at the clouds, overwhelmed by their beauty. What a Creator, I thought to myself. I felt led to praise God quietly in my heart. I became totally overwhelmed. Before I knew it, I was rousing myself from a trance-like state by singing spontaneously. The melody and words were foreign to me, yet in my spirit I perfectly comprehended their meaning. Over a year passed before someone finally explained to me that I had experienced the Holy Spirit in a special gift of rapture! I had sung a new song to the Lord with the gift of tongues and had been flooded with an incredible sense of God's presence, of joy and inner power.

But, gradually, I fell victim to a very subtle but serious malady. Like many I have known, I looked back at that moment as a special, and somehow isolated, event. While I continued to draw strength from that very exciting time, I did not continue to practice the presence of the Holy Spirit on a daily basis. Slowly, over a period of years, there was a cooling in my spirit and a feeling of distance between my daily life and the joyful rapture I felt that day on the airplane. I didn't stray from God in a rebellious or obvious way. It was much more subtle. I felt that my inner spiritual strength was leaking away. It all culminated four years ago as I contemplated the direction of my life. On the surface, everything seemed to be going extremely well. My concerts were always packed, I was able to effectively minister to the poor, my record albums were selling well, and there were no obvious problems in my life. Yet, I felt weak, spiritually flat. I realized I was not empowered anymore. Frighteningly, I felt I was not far from losing my faith! I prayerfully read over my journals and recalled the path by which God had led me and determined that I simply needed to "stir up the gift" of the Spirit within me. I had been waiting for something to happen to me rather than consciously choosing to be obedient. God may give us a gift, but we have to choose to reach out and accept it. It is an act of our will to receive a divine gift.

As a sheer act of will, I began to pray and to sing in the Spirit, and I continued on a daily basis. Praying in the Spirit is now a regular part of my life, and while the initial excitement of my early experience has admittedly subsided, I continue to feel a warmth and power which persists as long as I continue to stir up the Spirit and practice his presence daily.

Praise

An essential component of the empowering process we experience in the Holy Spirit is praise. As the psalmist says in Psalm 100, "Enter his gates with thanksgiving, his courts with praise." There is a mysterious kind of power present in praise which is capable of moving mountains! For example, controlling our thoughts at times seems almost impossible. And yet we know that a significant part of our sanctification must include the renewing of our minds. St. Paul says you must be "transformed by the renewal of your mind" and "acquire a fresh, spiritual way of thinking." As Jesus says, "From the mind stem evil designs . . . these are the things that make a man impure." There is a definite connection between the mind, our words, and our actions. As the Scriptures say, "What you think, you will become." Or as some people say, "Garbage in, garbage out."

I have found that it is only with the power of praise and thanksgiving that I can control and discipline my mind. Praise allows me to flood my consciousness with God, at which moment impure thoughts and fantasies must flee.

Thanksgiving

We are not only to be a people of praise, but also a people of *thanksgiving*. Let me share a personal example from my own life. I live in a Christian community. From the very beginning, we determined that we wanted to live an orderly life. But maintaining order can sometimes be difficult in domestic matters because we have all been raised differently and we bring so much of our own personal "baggage" into community life. These differences sometimes involve major issues. Usually, however, it's the little things that create problems. Believe me, it is not weighty, philosophical ideals that split communities. No, it's things like plates and bowls. To preserve order, our community decided to label our cupboards to separate such "important" things as plates and bowls. Now we are intelligent, God-centered people—we spend many hours a day worshiping God, praying, and reading the Scriptures, not to mention studying monastic history, church history, and theology. But, amazingly, we found that it was things like plates and bowls that split relationships!

One day I went to put away my bowl and, opening the cupboard, what did I find? Plates! That's right. Someone was putting plates in the bowl cupboard. And I was going to make it my business to find out just who it was. So I sat around the trailer in the morning with my cup of coffee and watched carefully. Sure enough, I saw it. Right in front of me, a certain individual took a bowl and put it in the plate cupboard.

An amazing psychological phenomenon began to take place in me. I started to observe this individual's behavior more closely. Certainly, I reasoned, if he was making mistakes in this area of his life, he was probably failing in other areas as well. Before I knew it, I began to look for all the bad things in that individual's life and, sure enough, I found them. As the little things began to bother me, I also began to realize that the relationship was dying. In fact, it was dead! It had to be reborn. It was my sin that had caused the problem. I had focused on the negative side of that person and had killed a valuable relationship—I think you know what I'm talking about.

As Christians, we are to be a Eucharistic people (the word Eucharist means "to give thanks"). In the kind of situation I have described above, thankfulness is the remedy. I had to begin to give thanks to God for that particular individual, to make a conscious and deliberate choice. God restored the relationship as a result.

We must have an "attitude of gratitude." It is in thanksgiving that we can put inflamed, critical attitudes back into an appropriate perspective, enabling us to more realistically deal with areas of difficulty.

We are asked to give God thanksgiving in everything. Even in the midst of trials. God actually wants us to give thanks when tragedies and evil befall us. That sounds crazy. It sounds dumb. But it's right there in the word of God. "Give thanks to God the Father always and for everything in the name of our Lord Jesus Christ." I believe it actually makes sense in the light of one other Scripture. It's the Scripture which says "all things work together for good for those who love God and those called according to his purpose." God doesn't tell us to thank him for evil. He didn't cause it. But we thank him for being Lord over every situation in our life, for bringing good out of evil. I know this is extremely difficult to believe. Can God actually protect us and make something good come out of every situation?

When Jesus was crucified, tortured to death, he cried out, "My God, my God, why have you forsaken me?" Jesus was hurting—he was in agonizing pain. But he also cried out, "Father, forgive them for they know not what they do." That took incredible faith! It also takes faith to cry out in thanksgiving even in the midst of our own personal crucifixions, which will inevitably come into our lives. Giving thanks will not take the pain out of our trials—there is no magical cure. Thanksgiving won't keep tragedies out of our lives, but it will provide incredible interior strength, something to keep us going when everyone else falls by the wayside in despondency and despair.

Singing praise and thanksgiving to the Lord will uplift your spirit with a buoyancy and power which may surprise you. It will change your life! It will modify the way you think, the way you speak, and the way you act. It will change everything for the better. This is nothing new, by the way. These are principles which re-emerge in spiritual renewal throughout the history of the church. Consider the following quote written by Augustine in the Roman Breviary: "Our thoughts in this present life should turn on the praise of God, because it is in praising God that we shall rejoice forever in the life to come. . . . Now therefore, brethren, we urge you to praise God. That is what we are telling each other when we say 'Alleluia.' You say to your neighbor, 'Praise the Lord!' and he says the same to you. . . . But see that you praise God not with your lips and voices alone, but with your mind, your lives and all your actions . . . as our ears hear each other's voices, so do God's ears hear our thoughts." Augustine confirms in this passage the power of praise in the renewing of our thoughts.

It is important to note that praise and thanksgiving should not be circumstantially based. When life is going perfectly and we feel on top of the world, praise and thanksgiving seem natural and appropriate. But it is in the worst of times that the real power of praise and thanksgiving emerges to confront the challenges we face. The prophet Habakkuk says, "For the fig trees have not fruit and no grape to grow on the vines, even though the olive crop fails and the fields produce no grain, even though the sheep all die and the cattle stalls are empty, I will be joyful and glad, because God is my savior." Therefore, even when life's blessings seem totally absent from us, we must still praise and thank God! It is an irony, a paradox, and a mystery. But it is also a spiritual fact of life.

Francis spoke of the principle of thanking God in all circumstances when he encouraged those who were sick: "I beg the friar who is sick to thank God for eveything; he should be content to be as God wishes him to be, in sickness or in health, because . . . God instructs in sickness and affliction and the spirit of compunction."

Tongues

In my own life, I express praise and thanksgiving best when I pray with the gift of tongues. To many, this practice is a controversial dimension of charismatic experience. Yet the Acts of the Apostles clearly shows that the phenomenon of tongues was an integral part of the gift of the Spirit to the church on Pentecost: "Tongues as of fire appeared, which parted and came to rest on each of them. All were filled with the Holy Spirit. They began to express themselves in foreign tongues and make bold proclamations as the Spirit prompted them."

Paul devotes much of his first letter to the Corinthians to the charismatic gifts of the Spirit. The gift of tongues is clearly evident in his writings: "There are different gifts of the same Spirit. . . . to each person the manifestation of the Spirit is given for the common good. . . . One receives the gift of tongues, another that of interpreting the tongues. . . . Set your heart on spiritual gifts. I should like it if all of you spoke in tongues. . . . Thank God I speak in tongues more than any of you." In this case, Paul was writing of the manifestation of tongues in the assembly of believers, emphasizing the need for interpretation and the preference for the gift of prophecy in order that the entire body might be edified. It is also clear, however, that speaking in tongues was an accepted part of the Corinthian worship.

Paul connects the praise of God with praying and singing in tongues. He says, "If I pray in a tongue, my spirit is at prayer but my mind contributes nothing. What is my point here? I want to pray with the spirit, and also to pray with my mind. I want to sing with my spirit and with my mind as well. If your praise of God is solely with the spirit, how will the one who does not comprehend be able to say 'Amen' to your thanksgiving?" In this case, both prayer and singing in the Spirit are linked to praise, thanksgiving, and the understanding of the mind.

The Psychology of Tongues, Thanksgiving, and Praise

Tongues, thanksgiving, and praise are linked together in a powerful dynamic which produces healing, freedom, power, and the kind of boldness required to bear witness to Christ in the preaching of the gospel. To deny this reality can stifle the Spirit. This is because even praise and thanksgiving can become a law for me. Jesus says, "You will know the truth and the truth will set you free." But Paul also says, "No one will be justified in God's sight through observance of the law; the law does nothing but point out what is sinful." Right as the law might be, I cannot fulfill it on my own. Again Paul says, "I do not do what I want to do but what I hate." The more I try to succeed, the more I fail. The more I fail, the more guilty I become. Ultimately, this will lead to despair. So the more I try to be righteous, the more I end up in a downward spiral of sin through failure. I can only reverse this downward spiral by praising God in a way that is beyond my thoughts. Even the concept of praise becomes a law for me. I cannot fulfill it. The more I try to fill my thoughts with God, the more I find thoughts of selfish distraction and darkness. Then I really feel guilty! The only way to control my thoughts is to temporarily bypass them. I allow my spirit and soul to go directly to God and let God, by his gift of grace, clean out my mind. Then I can fill my mind with God again.

But this is more than emotion. It is a choice. I choose to "stir up the gift" even when I don't feel like it. I pray in tongues by choice. This stirs up my emotions, for "Where your treasure is, there will your heart be also." So I rechannel my negative emotions by choice, and in the process cleanse my negative thoughts by the very positive powerful work of the Spirit.

Another powerful principle at work here is the power of the tongue. As Paul says, "Faith in the heart leads to justification, confession on the lips to salvation." As Jesus says, "Whoever says to this mountain, 'be lifted up and thrown into the sea,' and has no inner doubts but believes that what he says will happen, shall have it done for him." Or as the old proverb says, "From the lips flow both death and life." Thoughts affect actions and thoughts are solidified and expressed through words. Therefore, our words have a profound effect on both our thoughts and our actions.

So if we desire to temporarily bypass the "law" of objective thought in order to eventually cleanse our objective mind, then we might wish to speak subjective sounds in order to eventually cleanse the words of our lips. We speak in subjective praise, verbally, to reinforce subjective praise emotionally and mentally. We do this by choice. Then by God's power, not our own, God cleanses our heart, our mind, and our voices. It is a process that is psychologically sound and spiritually sure. That is why it was so universally evident in the early church.

Tears

Did you know that *tears* can be a tremendous spiritual gift from God? Sometimes tears are the only prayer a person is able to pray. These tears are precious in God's eyes. When Jesus went to dine at a Pharisee's home, a woman known throughout the town as a sinner approached him. Many believe her to have been a prostitute. As Jesus reclined at the table, "she brought in a vase of perfumed oil and stood behind him at his feet, weeping so that her tears fell upon his feet. Then she wiped them with her hair, kissing them and perfuming them with oil." As far as we know, this woman did not utter a single word. All she did was weep, wipe Jesus' feet with her hair, and kiss his feet. Jesus looked through her tears to her heart and said, "Her many sins are forgiven—because of her great love. . . . Your faith has been your salvation. Now go in peace."

In this case, the gift of tears is quite similar to that of tongues. Both express a deep eternal love and longing for Jesus that simply cannot be adequately expressed in spoken language. Tears can say more in a single moment than a thousand eloquent words, and they are perfectly understood by our loving Father.

Here again we see a kind of prayer that surpasses thoughts, working to free and renew the mind. In this way, tears may be very similar to stirring up the gift of tongues. Both are a choice and both include the mind but eclipse the capability of the mind. Both eventually free the mind of evil and replace it with the spiritual life of God.

Contriving or Controlling

It would be good to point out the difference between "contriving" and "controlling" these gifts. Paul says, "The spirit of the prophet is under the prophet's control," and "stir up the gift," but this should not be construed into contriving or faking spirituality. I am sure many of us have uncomfortable images of forced tongues and fake tears by well-meaning, but seriously misled zealots. Jesus says, "Worship God in spirit and in truth." It must be real! Gifts of love cannot be contrived.

But we do control our gifts and our emotions, especially when they so directly involve our emotions. God wants to involve our emotions through the gifts, but he does not want us to be controlled by our emotions. Thus, we may not feel like praising God, but we praise him anyway, believing by faith that "all things work together for good." We may not feel like using the gifts of God, but we do it anyway, believing by faith that it is for our good, the good of others, and the greater glory of God. Faith includes the emotions, but is not controlled by them. Faith is a decision. Inclusion of a godly emotional release is also a decision. In this sense, we do control the charismatic gifts. They can be chosen.

Let me be more specific in this regard. There are some who contrive God's gifts: Performers who can cry and weep on cue, charismatics who "teach" others how to speak in tongues, actually getting them to repeat certain sounds! In my opinion, this forcing and contriving is much like a lover forcing himself on his beloved.

On the other hand, there is a valid kind of teaching, of helping others to use these gifts. I do encourage people not to be afraid to make unintelligible sounds in private or in public. If they can't overcome their fear of looking foolish, they may never experience the gift. Likewise, I encourage praying in tongues even when people don't feel like it, believing that their emotions will follow the lead of a love decision. Otherwise, our praise of God and our entire faith would be subject to the whims of our feelings. Faith is, after all, an act of the will. Faith must include feelings, but it must not be controlled by them. Faith without feelings is dead, but feelings without faith are misdirected. Likewise, I think it is healthy to mentally stir up the image of God, Jesus, humankind, and ourselves, which lead us to godly tears. All of these methods control or channel emotions and gifts in the way of scriptural and traditional love and faith.

The history of the church is also full of amazing stories about rapture and ecstasy—states which have also been called being "slain in the Spirit." In particular, there are many stories about Francis of Assisi and his followers falling down before God as if dead, in rapt states of ecstasy which overpowered their physical beings. Frequently those who have experienced such extraordinary moments come away with a kind of empowerment, conviction, boldness, and burning love for God so that their entire lives are radically and permanently changed.

Reliance on the Spirit and the gifts he gives is evidenced even in the first chapter of *The Little Flowers of St. Francis.* "And just as those holy Apostles were for the whole world, marvels of holiness, filled with the Holy Spirit, so these most holy companions of St. Francis were men of such sanctity that the world has not had such wonderful and holy men from the times of the Apostles until now. For one of them was caught up to the third heaven like St. Paul, and that was Brother Giles. Another—tall Brother Philip—was touched on the lips by an angel with a burning coal, like Isaiah the prophet. Another—Brother Silvester, a very pure virginal soul—spoke with God as one friend with another, as Moses did. Another, by the keenness of his mind, soared up to the light of divine wisdom, like the eagle [John the Evangelist]—and this was the very humble Brother Bernard, who used to explain Holy Scripture in a most profound way."

We should welcome all the gifts of God which he provides through his Holy Spirit. We simply cannot afford to refuse any of them. Our attitude should be like that of Mary when she said, "Let it be done to me according to your word." At the same time, we must not pursue the spectacular, the mystical, or the miraculous with a sense of inappropriate curiosity or for the purpose of manipulation. Our motives must be pure, our desires must be to serve God with all our hearts. Let us not so much seek the gifts as the Giver.

There are many, I find, who do not desire to enter into the charismatic dimension of Christian life. Some feel they don't really need it—can we really be that certain that we aren't a terribly needy people? Many fear that this abandonment to God's will may require them to give up things which they would rather not release—can Christians really hold back areas of their life from God and be considered truly committed to their faith? A good number of people fear involvement in a kind of spirituality which can, and admittedly has in the past, been manipulative and unseemly. But must we miss out on a real, legitimate blessing of God because some others have been guilty of abuses?

I don't think we give ourselves that kind of intellectual, psychological permission. We would rather say that the charismatic renewal is great for those who really need it—I can even support it, in principle. But it's basically for others, not for me. This is a very common attitude. But as soon as we say that we will do anything for the Lord *except,* we are guilty of sin. I have heard people say, I will be a missionary, Lord; I will work for peace and social justice; I will join a religious order; I will do everything you ask me to do—but please, Lord, don't ask me to babble like an absolute idiot. As soon as "except" becomes acceptable, we have put a limitation on God and we are therefore not in total openness to his work in our lives.

Harboring selfishness and pride in our lives will prevent us from entering into the fullness of God's spiritual plan for his people. Pride is a devastating sin—the very root of evil. It was because of the sin of pride that the great angel, Lucifer, fell from grace. Because of pride, he became Satan, the archenemy of God, his own Creator.

We must humble ourselves and be willing to be "fools for Christ." This means becoming totally childlike, totally open to *whatever* God wants to give us. As Jesus says, "Unless you change and become like little children, you will not enter the kingdom of God." We must give ourselves this kind of mental permission. We must release ourselves from binding inhibitions which limit the spiritual freedom God intends for us.

This does not mean that all believers will speak in tongues or shed tears every time they pray. Yes, the Acts of the Apostles does depict the gift of tongues as accompanying almost every outpouring of the Holy Spirit on believers. Yes, it is true that Paul said, "I should like it if all of you spoke in tongues," and, "set your heart on spiritual gifts." And respected mystics such as Symeon the New Theologian do say that the gift and way of tears is possible for all believers. But all this must be seen in the balancing light of the Scriptures which say, "Are all apostles? Are all prophets? Are all teachers? Do all work miracles or have the gift of healing? Do all speak in tongues? Do all have the gift of interpretation?" The answer to this rhetorical question is no.

However, we must actively seek whatever gifts God wants to give us, yet be content with whatever we receive from him. God wants total openness. Too often we approach spiritual gifts with closed minds. As Paul says of the religious people of his day, "They make a pretense of religion but negate its power," or "they are always learning but never able to reach a knowledge of the truth." But Jesus says, "I have come that you might have life, and have it to the full." Jesus wants us to fulfill our potential as sons and daughters of God. We cannot do this with closed hearts and minds no matter how religious our reasons might seem.

Claim that which is your birthright as a child of God: the fullness of the Holy Spirit and his power for living a righteous, exemplary Christian life. Reach your potential as you mature in the things of the Spirit! Get to know God. Then make him known to our lost world. New power and boldness in the Spirit will enable you to bear witness to the love of Christ and his redemptive plan.

FIVE

Music Power: Worship, Thanksgiving, and Praise

O NCE YOU HAVE BEEN EMPOWERED by the Holy Spirit, you must learn how to channel that power and how to apply it. One way to release the power of the Spirit in our lives is through music. Music has been a very important part of the human experience from time immemorial. It has certainly been an important part of my life as a music minister and composer of sacred music. Some ancient Jewish traditions and writings teach that God created the universe by literally singing it into existence.

Music has been called the universal language. It is able to break through linguistic barriers and transcend cultural differences. It is almost like the gift of tongues because people may be deeply moved emotionally and spiritually by simply listening to, or participating in it. Music is also able to bypass the barriers of the mind to speak directly to the human heart. I believe this gift of music has been used by God to stir up that which is divine within the human soul.

When used in a liturgical context, music becomes a powerful tool for prayer. Augustine said, "He who sings, prays twice." Because music contains language in the form of lyrics, it can be at once theological, catechetical and meditational, carrying objective information. And, because it need not contain lyrics, the melody can be at the same time either charismatic or contemplative, carrying strong subjective meaning. Because music frequently involves both lyrics and melody, it can be an integration of all sacred things at once—a tremendously powerful medium of the Spirit. Music, therefore, can be highly sacramental, which simply means that it is an external medium which both effects and symbolizes that which is divine.

In many ways, music is *mystical,* beyond objective description, like a kiss between two lovers. It symbolizes the love they already possess, yet causes that love to grow even stronger, which is the idea behind a sacrament and the reason for sacred music. It symbolizes the faith of God's people. Music can be used by the Spirit to cause that faith and to deepen the work of the Spirit in our lives.

It is this sacramental, or mystical, dimension of musical art that makes it an icon in sound. The icon is a visual art which, ideally, is anointed by the Spirit in such a way that every person who beholds the icon is affected by the Spirit. The iconographer fasts and prays to this end, the whole time he or she is working on an icon. It is truly a sacred process. The same thing should happen in the interplay between the musician, his or her art, and the listener. In this sense, we are called to be composers and performers of truly sacred music.

Throughout the Scriptures we find God using music to accomplish his purposes. One of the greatest examples of this is a case in the Old Testament where music takes on both charismatic and liturgical dimensions: charismatic because the power of the Holy Spirit descends on a people; liturgical because it is within the established levitical order that the music emerges to produce God's special presence. Take a look at 2 Chronicles 5. King Solomon had finally completed the Temple and the elders of Israel gathered together in Jerusalem to bring the Ark of the Covenant from the Citadel of David in a special celebration during which time the Lord would take possession of his new dwelling place. Levitical cantors were playing cymbals, harps, and lyres while 120 priests played trumpets. Singers gave glory to God and praised him, singing, "He is good, for his love is everlasting."

During this event a great cloud filled the Temple—God's glory and his presence filled the place, overwhelming the people of God. The Scriptures actually say that the priests were so overcome they could no longer perform their duties!

We see here how music ministry can play an essential part in worship, and we also can observe that when God's presence is ushered into a worship situation, we are sometimes overwhelmed to the point that we can no longer perform.

Imagine that! The audacity of God to interrupt the sacred liturgy! But I firmly believe he wants to do the same today. He wants to "interrupt" our lives to shower his presence upon us in power and in glory. He desires to open us up to all that he has for us when we worship him (even though a football game is scheduled to begin on TV in an hour or two!).

In the above passage of Scripture, we read about the cloud—a symbol of God's presence but also a symbol of transfiguration. Remember the transfiguration of Jesus on Mount Tabor. God wants to bring the cloud of transfiguration into our own lives. He wants conversion. In the same way that the priests and musicians summoned the presence of God through their celebration of music, God wants to usher us into a personal love relationship with himself. Music can help us initiate this process of conversion to Christ—and to sustain the momentum of movement toward him.

Structure and Freedom

It is important to remember that we must have both structure and creativity—*form and freedom*. We need the liturgy, but we also need the heart, the soul, and the emotion of liturgical worship. We need rules but we also need inspiration. Music can provide both structure and freedom in worship because, in the same way that a human body has a heart and a skeletal structure, music has the ability to inspire an emotional response while operating according to established musical structure and theory.

In my experience, I find that Catholics often think that the Spirit of God is present only when the sacraments are present. Protestants, on the other hand, often feel the presence of the Spirit only when the pastor preaches. I find that both concepts are one-sided. When the structure of liturgy and the freedom of the Spirit are both present, then worship is greatly enhanced. Music, when properly and expertly introduced into worship, can meet both of these needs.

Call down the cloud of God's presence in your own life. Let his transfiguring power overwhelm you and move you deeper into true Christian conversion, whether you are a music minister or a worshiper in the congregation. All of God's people can participate.

Prophetic and Evangelistic

Music can also be *prophetic and evangelistic* as we see in 1 Samuel 10. This passage describes the anointing of Saul as king of Israel. Prophets and musicians, preceded by lyres, tambourines, flutes, and harps, fell into an ecstatic state before Saul, which had been earlier prophesied. Saul was drawn into this rapturous experience and was changed. The Scriptures say that the people were amazed. Music was not only a part of this prophetic process, but it also played a role in Saul's conversion—music became a tool of evangelism. The Scripture says that Saul was changed.

Over the past number of years I have received countless letters from brothers and sisters in Christ who tell me that one of my songs brought them into relationship with God. I am always rewarded by this and extremely humbled at the same time. To think that one of my recordings, or a song I performed in concert, could have the power to produce conversion is truly an awesome concept. It is a sobering responsibility and privilege which I take very seriously. It is a concept I hope to transmit to you as you seek to be empowered to serve God in every area of your life.

As a Franciscan, I am always interested in how St. Francis, and those around him, were influenced by music. In the Legend of Perugia, Section 43, we learn how St. Francis, after many trials, was led by God to praise him by offering thanks and praises for his creation. This is when the "Canticle of the Sun" was written as an inspiring, high praise to God in the midst of God's created world. Not only did the song prove to be inspiring to Francis and his followers when they were experiencing their own tribulations, but the song was used when the friars went out to evangelize the world. Their desire was to "move men's hearts," and they accomplished this through preaching and through song.

Music is also a powerful spiritual force in deliverance. Again, look at 1 Samuel 16 where King Saul was tormented by an evil spirit. He was overcome by a kind of dark depression which was, at times, manifested in melancholy and violence. David, a skilled harpist, was summoned to play music for the king, calming him. Amazingly, when the music was played, the powers of darkness lifted—spiritual power was released through the skill of a young musician, a musician who would one day be king and continue to use songs and praises throughout his life. Because of David's obedience to his call, his psalms became a significant part of the Scriptures, a rich deposit of biblical wealth which continues to bless God's people thousands of years later.

A Tool for a Holy Life

Ephesians 4 and 5 illustrates how music bears on *lifestyle and praise* in the church. Here we find Paul addressing a long list of problems among members of the Christian community at Ephesus, which had come to his attention. Serious sin was being committed—the kind of sin which we continue to deal with in the church to this day. Paul admonished the church, through his letter, against theft, anger, bitterness, spitefulness, fornication, promiscuity, impurity, coarse talk, idolatry, works of darkness, drunkenness; the list goes on. Paul was calling the individual members of the church to change, to be truly converted. He forcefully urged them to awaken from their sleep, to rise from the dead and allow Christ to shine on them once again.

But how were they to accomplish this ongoing conversion? Paul told the people of the Ephesian church community to "be filled with the Holy Spirit, addressing one another in psalms, hymns and inspired songs. Sing praise to the Lord with all your heart and give thanks to God the Father always and for everything in the name of our Lord Jesus Christ."

How does Paul think that such serious sin can be overcome through mere singing? Isn't that a bit naive? Paul understood that changed lives are the result of changed thoughts. Evil thoughts, when allowed to fester in our minds, will always produce evil. Meditation on good thoughts, however, will ultimately produce good in our lives. When we sing, or when we listen to edifying music, the melody and the lyrics will fill our minds objectively and subjectively with goodness and peace. This kind of meditation will ultimately overcome evil with good and, when engaged appropriately and frequently, will continue God's wondrous process of conversion in our lives. Paul understood the great mystery of human thought and its consequences. Apparently, he also understood the liberating role which music could play in conforming our thoughts, and therefore our lives, to Christ.

But we must do more than just sing notes and words. We must move beyond performance to worship. Paul said, "I want to sing with my spirit and with my mind as well." St. Francis cautioned his brothers, "Do not concentrate on the melody of the chant, but be careful that your hearts are in harmony so that your words may be in harmony with your hearts and your hearts with God. Your aim should be to please God by purity of heart, not to soothe the ears of the congregation by your sweet singing."

Musical Styles

Now that we have looked at the way God has used music in various areas of the Scriptures, let's take a look at musical styles and orientation. I have been playing musical instruments, singing, and writing songs for almost twenty years. I have played, and have been exposed to, a wide range of musical styles both secular and Christian. I find that in today's world of contemporary Christian music there are two primary orientations: entertainment-oriented ministry and ministry-oriented entertainment. Both kinds of music will minister and both will entertain. The emphasis, however, will vary depending upon the artist, his style and purpose in composing or playing the music in question.

Some Christians contend that music should never be used for entertainment. They say that we should only listen to Christian music and only certain kinds of Christian music at that! But I believe that all human beings, Christians included, have a legitimate need for entertainment. Even the most serious of Christians need occasional diversion, recreation, and renewal. Music, sacred or secular, may be a healthy way to renew the inner person. However, we shouldn't overlook the fact that there is real danger in today's music. Much of the music that we hear is morally unacceptable. Just listen to the lyrics. Music is a powerful force that affects both mind and spirit. So care should be taken in the selection of the music we expose ourselves to. Most contemporary Christian music is Christian entertainment, and that's okay. It is not intended to carry a heavy theological message or a deep meditational focal point. It is a healthy diversion, and it can be very healthy fun. Such music is a clear example of entertainment-oriented ministry.

Bonaventure mentions entertainment-oriented art forms in

his work, "Retracing the Arts to Theology": "Art (mechanical or dramatic) is either a consolation or a comfort; it is either directed against a sorrow or a need; or again is either useful or entertaining. As Horace says, 'Poets aim either to serve or to please,' and also 'He draws all applause who adjoins the useful and the sweet.' If the purpose of an art is to afford consolation and entertainment, this will be dramatic art, or plays, embracing every kind of performance, singing, instrumental music, fiction, or choreography." Bonaventure's words show that the question of Christian involvement in entertainment-oriented art is not new, and despite many warnings against its misuse, entertainment-oriented art has not always been viewed as an evil thing in and of itself.

Today, the church, while asserting the potential goodness of such art, also warns concerning "the connection between what is called art and the rights and norms of moral law. The increasing disputes on this subject frequently spring from ethical and artistic theories which are false. Hence, the Council asserts that the primacy of the objective moral order demands absolute allegiance." Thus, *true Christian morality always takes priority* over the use of any art form, no matter how technically good it appears to be.

Ministry-oriented entertainment, on the other hand, focuses on ministry but must, to some degree, be entertaining. A good speaker, for example, must be able to entertain the listener in order to enhance his or her message and hold attention. Entertainment is a component of communication which can be extremely useful. This is why I believe that music which is created to minister must be good. It must be composed and played with real expertise and, to some degree, have entertainment value. We might be aware of "keeping our audience," but this does not mean that we use manipulative techniques. I can remember in my rock'n'roll days, that we always started and ended our concerts with fast, hard-driving rock'n'roll songs. This approach was carefully calculated to leave the audience with the general impression of a quick-paced, fun evening. Audiences will often remember your first song and the song which closed the show. However, they inevitably forget much of what was in the middle. This is a show-biz entertainment technique. However, this kind of manipulation should never be carried over as an end in itself in Christian music.

Quite often our ministry-oriented music is geared to evangelization. When this is the case, the music should be performed well and it should be culturally attuned. A truly global approach to Christian music should use the expression of a particular culture to reach that culture. However, we should not use a cultural expression only for the sake of culture. That is worldly. Furthermore, some expressions are morally incompatible with the gospel in light of their distorted emphases. In spite of the condemnation of certain Christian leaders, even "rock'n'roll" can sometimes be an appropriate expression when ministering in today's world. I relearned this myself during a recent trip to the Philippines. In America, I am known for my worship music which is quiet, meditational, and classical sounding. I can do a three-hour concert and hear a pin drop. In the Philippines, however, there was a certain restlessness in the audiences. These were frequently Christian audiences. They wanted to be ministered to, but they had a certain cultural expectation. They love fun, up-tempo music. As I began to sense the cultural needs of the people, I began to play a few more up-tempo songs and even one or two numbers from my first Christian album, complete with hot guitar licks! The response was overwhelming! In the end, I was able to lead the people to praise, worship, and real meditation, but it required what for me was a radical shift in musical strategies. As music ministers, we must always be aware of the needs of the listener while at the same time allowing the Spirit to lead.

However, I would caution against "Christian rock'n'roll." The term "rock'n'roll" is an ethnic sexual term. While it no longer means this, it does reveal the original intention of the very nature of much of the music. The Christian might play "contemporary" music, and it might have a beat. But it cannot be pure "rock'n'roll."

Quite often Christian music, whether entertainment-oriented or ministry-oriented, can be powerfully prophetic. On the entertainment side we see such secular artists as Bob Dylan and even groups like U-2 singing powerfully and effectively about injustice, human alienation from God, war, and other social commentary. On the ministry side we will sometimes find artists whose lyrics may overpower the melody in such a way as to downplay entertainment. Both are legitimate expressions depending on the audience and the purposes of the artist.

Again, an example from the life of St. Francis may serve to illustrate the point. At a time when Francis was very sick, the bishop of Assisi excommunicated the chief magistrate of the town and a bitter feud arose between them which became known throughout the entire area. Francis grieved over this conflict and, even in the midst of his illness, wrote another verse to his "Canticle of the Sun":

All praise be yours, my Lord,
Through those who grant pardon for love of You;
Through those who endure sickness and trial.
Happy those who endure in peace;
By You, Most High, they will be crowned.

Francis called upon his companions to sing the canticle in the presence of the bishop and the chief magistrate. With some reluctance, they came together in order to hear the verse which they knew Francis had written for them. At the end of the song, they wept and cried out, embracing one another, "with much tenderness and affection." Here, in the midst of social conflict, a simple servant of God composed a piece of music which shattered the enmity which existed between two powerful leaders. How prophetic! What would happen today if Spirit-filled musicians and singers were to bring forth the kind of music which could reconcile warring groups?

Sometimes music should be more meditative, almost like music therapy. I happen to be an honorary member of a group of therapists who are practicing Christians. Many of them use my music as therapy for their patients. Meditative music can be performed in a kind of minimalist style, much like some of my recent recordings without lyrics. This may be the kind of music which David played for a troubled Saul and the kind of music which comforted St. Francis as he lay near death, wracked with illness. "To comfort his soul and ward off discouragement in the midst of his grave and serious infirmities, he often had the brothers sing for him the 'Praises of the Lord' which he had previously composed during his sickness" (Omnibus of Sources).

Let us also consider music in light of scientific theory and research concerning the phenomenon of brain wave frequencies. When we are conscious and functioning in normal daily activities, our brain waves move more quickly. When we sleep, for instance, they move more slowly. It is a scientific fact that our deepest self comes out in dreams when our brain waves are moving very slowly. Likewise, whatever we put into our mind at this point makes a major imprint on our deepest consciousness.

Our brain waves also move very slowly during meditation or prayer. That is why it is so vitally important to follow the scriptural admonition to "meditate on the law of the Lord day and night." What we put into our minds during prayer gets deep into our very souls. It has definite effects on our thoughts, our feelings, our words, and eventually even our actions.

The phenomenon of slow brain waves also happen when we listen to music. That is why it is so important to listen only to what Paul calls "all that is true, all that deserves respect, all that is honest, pure, admirable, decent, virtuous, or worthy of praise." If we listen to aggressive and violent music, we program aggression and violence into our souls. If we listen to immoral lyrics, we program immorality into our minds. These things tend to come through rock and roll, but they are also very prevalent in the story lines of country music. They are also present in the many seemingly respectable operas of the musical greats and even in the very soul of the composer coming through the emotionally stirring melodies and harmonies of his or her work. These are not harmless; they affect the reality of our minds, our hearts, and our souls.

Of course, this warning can lead to an unhealthy separatism. On one hand, we must "come out of Babylon"; on the other, we must "be in the world, not of it." We must recognize the beauty, truth, and goodness that comes to us through all creation, fallen though it may be. This includes all forms of secular music. We should learn from all that is good in it and praise God for it. But we should also learn to sift it through the cleansing blood of Christ and the Word of God. Then we can say with St. Paul "everything God has created is good. Nothing is to be rejected when it is received with thanksgiving, for it is made holy by God's word and by prayer." Therefore, all music can be received but only after it has been baptized in Christ.

So the converse of the warning is also true. If we sing only praises to God, if we sing his word, if we listen to and sing only music that is good and beautiful and true and gives glory to God, we will receive extra power to become more Christlike.

Music which produces worship is the most challenging of all. We are to worship in "Spirit and in truth," in "Spirit and reality." This worship brings us into a relationship with Jesus Christ which is honest and real. That is what worship is for. It is the final end: honest relationship with God. Music which assists in deliverance or meditation accomplishes something which is part of the process. Music which teaches or is prophetic informs or challenges us for a higher purpose. But worship is not, like these, a step along the path. It is the goal, the end, the be-all in our relationship with God. That is why worship music is so vitally important.

In worship music our emotions must be involved. We are the bride of Christ. We are in a marriage relationship with him, and in a true love relationship, emotions must be expressed.

Worship music must therefore take into account the role that emotions play in embracing God, in losing ourselves in him. We must be naked before him as his bride. We must be honest. We must be real.

Worship music is therefore an art form. I would even say it is the highest expression of musical art. Art is the communication of an interior reality through an external medium. The artistic dimensions of our worship music must convey this interior reality in much the same way that the sacraments are an external sign of an interior truth. Worship music must also therefore be sacramental in itself in that it symbolizes and effects God's grace. Worship involves a wide array of human emotions. Therefore, a wide array of musical styles must be used to symbolize and stir these emotions. The actual style is not central. Worship is central. The human experience of God is central. Style is only a tool. Worship music may, at times, be a form of rock music. In this context, the worship is expressed in great power and force demonstrating the majesty of God. Listen, for example, to a heavy metal rock song. You may find, to your amazement, that it is not that dissimilar, in effect, to choruses of Handel's "Messiah." Both are booming and overpowering. When used with expertise they can exhilarate and uplift the worship experience. Worship music may also be, of course, classical, which also expresses great power and artistic sensitivity. It can involve the pristine clarity of Vivaldi to demonstrate the orderly perfection of God. It can involve the outward rippling and geometrical "imperfection" of Ravel's impressionism, to demonstrate God's revelation in creation. It can involve the new minimalism to demonstrate the otherworldliness of meditation and contemplation. It will speak of the elegance and sophistication of the Lord, elevating our minds and spirits into union with him.

Gregorian Chant is able to do something which rock and classical music simply cannot do. It is extremely contemplative, a kind of mystical prayer to God. Gregorian chant dates to the

9th century, and for centuries afterward this form was the most highly regarded standard of liturgical music. It secured forever the important role of music in church worship.

If you are a music minister or even a professional musician, you must be aware that worship music may take all of the above forms at one time or another, and you should seek to expand your range of appreciation to encompass them, broadening your own musical vocabulary and reaching more areas in the lives of those who are touched by your work. I, myself, intentionally listen to and study many different musical disciplines so I might almost naturally integrate and synthesize them together in the music I compose and record. If you are not musically inclined, you will nevertheless gain more insight into your own ability to worship as you come to understand various dimensions and components that worship music may take. You also should seek to listen to, and become fluent in, different forms of music which will motivate and enhance your own worship experience. Remember, we are not all called to be musicians and singers. Very frankly, I feel that those who do not possess the real musical talent, along with the acquired skills, do a disservice to the body of Christ by attempting to gain positions of leadership in Christian music. Gideon's army numbered only a very few, but they were called for a vast and overwhelming victory. You must discern your call, pray, work, and seek artistic maturity.

I would like to say a word about art in general from a Franciscan perspective. As is said of St. Francis: "In every work of the artist, he praised the Divine Artist," and of St. Bonaventure: "What he is saying, in short, is that in art as well as Scripture and nature, the image of the Creator may be discerned." This concept is highly sacramental and places art on a high level of revelation of the eternal when properly produced, perceived, and used.

While the particular call to music ministry is only for some, congregational singing is universally for all. You may not think you are a singer. Indeed, you may not possess the talent, but don't let that keep you from fully experiencing the wonder of God's grace in worship as you raise your voice to him along with other brothers and sisters. I guarantee you that the voices of professionals and non-professionals joined together in praise of God creates a harmony much more pleasing to God than the best choir or orchestra. It is the harmony of love among God's people. This is the highest art.

SIX

Staying Power: Community and Personal Discipline

A S WE DISCUSSED IN THE LAST CHAPTER, music can be an enormous channel of blessing when it releases the power of the Spirit in the church and in our individual lives. Some forms of Christian music, such as Gregorian Chant or Handel's "Messiah," have been with us for ages and will doubtless endure to the end of time. They have what we might call staying power.

Why is this? Music like this has staying power not only because it is technically excellent, but because it is centered in the eternal, transcendent value of Christian faith. On the other hand, we need only look around at our Top 40, three-minute, hit singles in order to see that a song may be here today, gone tomorrow. True, today's music can unleash enormous forces— for good and for evil—but the brevity of a song's acceptance is astounding! We live in a throw-away world, a world of transience, a world of change and a world of novelty.

Sadly, this is true of contemporary Christian music as well. In my ten years as a Christian artist, I have seen large numbers of Christian musicians, and their songs, come and go. Much of this trend appears to be the direct result of the commercialization of Christian music, which tends to rise and fall with the whims of the marketplace. I believe, however, that Christian artists who are deeply centered in their sacred musical vocation, and on Christ as their foundation, will endure through the mercurial ups and downs of prevailing commercial trends and fickle consumer tastes. Staying power requires consistent, enduring commitment to Christ, on whom our lives must be totally centered. As I have said so often: my being is not centered on my ministry. My ministry flows out of my being. And my being can only find balance and eternal meaning in Christ and his church.

A few years back I learned some of the toughest lessons of my life as a Christian. After the high energy excitement and elation of my charismatic experience began to dissipate, I was left with a kind of spiritual depression, a feeling of drifting in my faith (and nearly out of my faith). As I mentioned earlier, I experienced a spiritual crisis and began to wonder about my situation. I realized I was going through what John of the Cross called "the dark night of the soul," and, like others, I began to understand that I should not seek the joy of my charismatic experience, for it would surely elude me if it became the object of my pursuit. I had to seek Christ and him alone, even in the darkness and the pain of uncertainty and confusion. We are not promised, even in renewal, a never-ending spiritual picnic but rather we are promised the cross and we are asked to bear it daily in a sacrificial commitment to Jesus. It is often here, in the darkest of places, that we find the true joy of resurrection, the true power of God, and real staying power.

I would add a brief word of warning about depression. As Christians we must be careful not to judge too quickly. Our depression may not result from sin, drifting spirituality, or personal laziness. It can very commonly result from a psychological or biochemical condition. When prayer, praise, and worship do not seem to help, the depressed person should feel perfectly free to seek sound medical advice. He or she could be suffering from a nutritional imbalance, stress, exhaustion, the lack of counseling, or perhaps even lack of medication. It is important to maintain the balance between spirituality and the pragmatic dimensions of wise day-to-day living.

Community Power

A phenomenon I have found to be most dangerous to the rooted, consistent Christian life is our near cultic focus on personalities. As Americans, we seem to be infatuated with stardom, fame, fortune, and personalities in general. But human beings, imperfect as we are, will certainly fall. We all have feet of clay, and we must never put our primary spiritual focus on any individual. Charismatic leaders, sooner or later, are sure to tumble from their pedestals. Unfortunately, they frequently take a good number of well-intentioned people with them. This is painfully evident in the wake of the television evangelist scandals we have witnessed lately.

I remember a particular church which, in the wake of the charismatic renewal and under the guidance of an extra-ordinarily gifted pastor, was growing and reaching out to the community in an exciting way. Sunday morning church attendance swelled beyond the capacity of the sanctuary; Sunday school classes were jammed and the people were inspired greatly by their pastor who possessed a true gift of communication. Then tragedy struck. The pastor fell into serious sin and left the ministry. Almost overnight the church fell apart. Attendance was down, bills were left unpaid and the sheep were scattered. It is most important that we keep our eyes on Christ, that we center ourselves in him. Otherwise, putting people on spiritual pedestals can involve a subtle form of idolatry.

In the time immediately following Christ's ascension, the Holy Spirit was poured out in great power and the early church grew in an explosion of evangelism. Unquestionably, those were exciting times. But persecution was also a reality and the infant church needed to develop stability, real staying power.

We know that fellowship became very important in maintaining the life of the church. The concept of community developed early in the life of the church and has continued to this day. But what is Christian community? Certainly it must be more than just sitting in pews on a Sunday morning. It must be a cohesive, social force which, when confronted with crises, such as the one mentioned above, will continue in commitment to common goals and actually be strengthened as a result of trials and tribulations.

The early Christian community is depicted in Acts 2:42-47:

> These remained faithful to the teaching of the apostles, to the brotherhood, to the breaking of bread and to the prayers. The many miracles and signs worked through the apostles made a deep impression on everyone. The faithful all lived together and owned everything in common; they sold their goods and possessions and shared out of the proceeds among themselves according to what each one needed. They went as a body to the Temple every day but met in their houses for the breaking of the bread; they shared their food gladly and generously; they praised God and were looked up to by everyone. Day by day the Lord added to their community those destined to be saved.

This passage of Scripture is loaded with qualities found in the Christian community: faithfulness to apostolic teaching, the breaking of the bread, prayer disciplines, common quarters, shared ownership, the selling of possessions, sharing with those in need, charismatic manifestations, corporate worship and praise. These components of communal Christian life provided the strength and consistency which would be required to see the church through two millenia. These community concepts are just as relevant today as they were then, even though they sometimes don't fit easily into our Western cultural expectations. Recently, however, some new forms of Christian community, among them intentional communities known as basic Christian communities, have begun to emerge. The "basic community" movement finds Christians coming together in order to share their faith in the study of Scriptures, the breaking of bread and sharing common prayer, among other things.

The 1986 Catholic document, "Instruction on Christian Freedom and Liberation," speaks of basic communities:

> The new basic communities or other groups of Christians which have arisen to be witnesses to this evangelical love are a source of great hope for the Church. If they really live in unity with the local church and the universal Church, they will be a real expression of communion and a means of constructing a still deeper communion.

Practical forms of the basic Christian communities evolved among Hispanics in the Americas who found that they played a key role in Catholic church renewal:

> A revitalized sense of fellowship fills the Church in Latin America, Africa, Europe and Asia with pastoral joy and hope. The Synod of Bishops in 1974 witnessed an outpouring of such hope from Latin American pastors, who saw in basic Christian communities a source of renewal in the Church. Since these communities are a proven benefit of the Church, we highly encourage their development. The basic Christian community is neither a discussion or study group nor parish. It is "the first and fundamental ecclesiastical nucleus, which on its own level must make itself responsible for the richness and expansion of the faith, as well as of the worship of which it is an expression." It should be an expression of a Church that liberates from personal and structural sins; it should be a small community with personal relationships; it should form part of a process of integral evangelization; and it should be in communion with other levels of the Church.

Unquestionably, Spirit power, Christian renewal, and staying power relate closely to the concept of Christian community. There are many valid expressions of community already in the Catholic church, and the church herself encourages all people to be open to new forms which the Spirit may raise up in our own times. Whether these diverse expressions of community take on such forms as Franciscan, Dominican, Benedictine, lay communities, religious, charismatic communities, or more traditional expressions, they must all share some essential elements in common.

We live in a time when social stability is deteriorating, particularly in the West. We are entering into a more transient phase as a nation when many profound changes are happening very quickly. In times past we lived a more settled, localized life. Before there were giant cities, advanced means of transportation, or modern communications, life was much simpler. We knew many of our neighbors and fellow citizens on a first name basis. While these weren't overtly Christian communities, most of the people in these small towns and villages were Christians and generally interacted on Christian principles. They frequently worshiped together in local parishes or churches and supported one another in many other areas of life. It is obvious that in today's fast-moving world our society is losing the communal solidarity of earlier generations.

More than ever we must rediscover and implement the concept of Christian community. The Franciscan document, "I Have Done My Part, May Christ Teach You Yours," says:

> We live in a society torn apart everywhere; we see all around us discord on every level—within the family, and individual nations and between nations. Whether these conflicts stem from genuine difficulties in reconciling radically different approaches, or whether (as is more likely) they are simply a manifestation of insatiable greed, our role as Franciscans is helping to resolve and to clear. We are to show forth with unmistakable clarity the love for one another enjoined on us

in the Gospels: "By this will all know that you are my disciples, if you have love for one another" (John 13:35). "Community" is the name given to our lifestyle as Franciscans, called as we are to live together in supernatural love and to support one another in our common efforts and discern and fulfill the will of God. So many things are implied in that name: the ideal of equality, combining our individual charisms in the service of others, the joy of living together with brothers and sisters, mutual care and kindness, enthusiasm in the faithful discharge of our duties, joyful encouragement of one another in the spirit of sacrifice; all these make our Franciscan community the very special presence of the Church on earth and a foretaste for all people everywhere of the glorious kingdom of heaven.

The diagram below demonstrates the kind of support Christians and Christian families must have, under God, in order to survive, grow, and share Christ with a needy world.

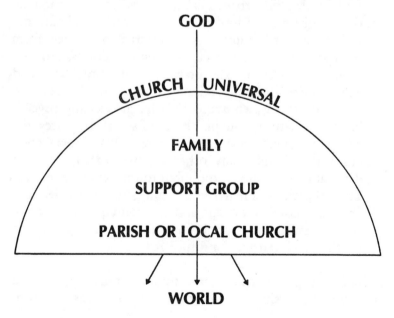

In the hierarchy of spiritual values, of course, God must be at the top. Below God is the worldwide Christian family—the church universal which includes everything we are about as Christians. Then we have a particular expression of church, the natural nuclear family which is actually the most basic and earliest form of Christian community. The support group is the next expression of community. It should be large enough to provide security but small enough to allow for real personal relationships to grow. Jesus' choice of twelve apostles has been seen as the ideal example of a support group. This kind of support should assist individuals as well as Christian families. In turn, support groups may be found within local churches or parishes. Today, social turmoil is taking its most significant toll on the family unit. When the family is compromised, the overall effectiveness of the church in communicating the gospel is tremendously weakened.

The above-mentioned Franciscan document puts it like this:

> Still another disturbance is the deterioration of the relationship between a husband and his wife—a relationship which has lost the important support it once drew from traditional values. Changed working conditions, growing economic insecurity, the prevalence of materialistic and hedonistic philosophies, relaxed moral standards, the labor-saving devices which abound today, the ensuing psychological immaturity, the instability of social structures, the unrelenting pressure exerted by new means of social communication, and many other factors (often not even detectable) conspire all too often to threaten married life. The obligations of marriage are soft-pedaled, married love becomes more precarious and the consequences are obviously destructive, not only for couples themselves but also for their children and for future generations.

The message is quite obvious: support for marriage and the family is diminishing in today's world. The weakened condition of the family ultimately weakens the church and society at large. Local churches and parishes, which should be supportive of the family, are simply too large in most cases to care for the pressing needs of individual members. Smaller, more manageable groups are therefore needed to play supportive roles. As the church document on basic communities says, these groups should be more than just prayer meetings or Bible studies—they must be *intentional* Christian communities.

As the rule of the Secular Franciscan Order emphasizes, "By living the grace of matrimony, husbands and wives in particular should be a witness in the world to the love of Christ for His church." And in the whole human family, "They should cultivate the Franciscan spirit of peace, fidelity and respect for life, striving to make it a sign of a world already renewed in Christ." Thus does this time-tested Franciscan expression of basic community emphasize and support the more primary expression of Christian community in the Christian family. Christian family life is a priority often overlooked by communities which demand too much time for communal activites, depriving needed time for the family. I personally do not suggest more than one or two nights a week for community activity. The rest should be left for the family.

Community, however, cannot be established and maintained without commitment. This commitment usually takes the form of a vow, promise, or some sort of covenant, either temporary or permanent.

Commitment is yet one more important value which has eroded in today's relativistic world. Not long ago a young man came to our prayer community in hopes of becoming a permanent member. It became apparent to him how crucial commitment is in maintaining community, yet he seemed unable to fully grasp or live within the ideal of enduring commitment. Because he came from a home which was shattered by divorce, he finally concluded that commitment was a concept he could not relate to. Nothing had been settled or concretely anchored in his life as a young person. As the family fragmented, any sense of commitment he had developed was destroyed. His story serves as a tragic illustration supporting the Christian community concept. Had this young man and his family been supported by loving Christians, it is quite possible that they would have endured the trials and stresses which ultimately took their tragic toll. Had he learned commitment, he could have completed the support cycle by living in a supportive community, a community which could go on to support other families.

There are six basic building blocks which I believe are absolutely essential to the establishment and maintenance of any Christian community. If any one of them is missing, the community will be anemic, its existence threatened.

1. *Apostolic Instruction*: The community must have sound leadership. Catholics believe that leadership must be properly linked to church authority. The church authorizes the leaders to provide the kind of guidance and instruction required to direct the community. This provides a healthy check and balance against leadership too lax or too dictatorial, which can be the case in communities isolated from the larger church.

Of course, the Scriptures will play an important guiding role, but they cannot play the only role. The "sola scriptura" approach to authority in the community will result in divisions as each member interprets the Scriptures in different ways. Remember that the early church community in Jerusalem, which was so dynamic and explosive in its growth, did not have our Bible! In fact, the Scriptures emerged from the church, not the other way around.

Therefore, Catholics believe it is vitally important to interpret Scripture in light of apostolic authority which may be found in the earliest writings of the church by the church Fathers. If there is a particular debatable passage of Scripture dividing the church or the community today, it only makes sense to go back to the church from which the Scriptures came to see if we can find at least a substantial agreement among members and leaders. If we can, we can apply their interpretation of that debatable passage to our situation today, in a developed way. When we do this we make great steps towards unity and balance. Apostolic teaching balanced with Scripture will greatly assist any community in maintaining equilibrium and in avoiding extremist tendencies.

2. *Prayer:* Of course, prayer must be considered a vital building block in any Christian community. For example, the early church in Jerusalem seems to have prayed structured, liturgical prayers as a community but not to the negation of the full operation of the gifts of the Holy Spirit. Prayer will take on different forms in different situations. For example, public prayer will take place with the group together. It is quite possible that public prayers will be, at times, liturgical and more structured, and at other times devotional and perhaps charismatic in nature. There will also be times of private prayer. Private prayer may also be structured as it is read from various established sources; it may be devotional or, again, charismatic. You will remember from our "music power" chapter that we discussed form and freedom. Whether public or private, prayer within the Christian community context must combine both established form and true freedom for a balanced community prayer agenda.

3. *Eucharist:* Communion, or Eucharist, cannot be over-emphasized in its importance for Christians, especially those living in community. Celebration of the Eucharist moves community members beyond the cold intellectual understanding of Christ, takes us beyond the fluctuating emotional experience of Christ, and moves us into a mystical, sacramental place in the very heart of Christ in a way that is constant, steady and true—a way bigger than our

individual experience, but inclusive of it—a way that both signifies and affects the unity of the whole church. Eucharist becomes a point of unity where Jesus plays the central role in our individual lives and in the life of the community.

St. Francis said that when the apostles looked upon Jesus with the eyes of flesh, they saw a man. When they looked upon him with eyes of faith, they saw God incarnate. Likewise, he stated, when we look upon the Eucharist with eyes of flesh, we merely see bread and wine. But when we look upon the Eucharist with eyes of faith, we see the presence of Jesus in our midst! The same may be said of community. When we look upon community with eyes of flesh, we will see its many problems, challenges, difficulties. Our sinful humanity is all too evident. But when we look at community with eyes of faith, we will find Christ in all realities of communal life together. As Jesus was both man and God, we will begin to see his divine presence in the midst of our human struggles and community. Thus, the Eucharistic model helps us to see all created things in a divinely transformed manner. Through the Eucharist, and all that it represents, we can change our concept of life to one of faith and sacramental fullness.

Communities that contain both Protestant and Catholic members will, no doubt, experience the pain that comes from not being able to partake of the Eucharist together. But is this pain always bad? If Communion is supposed to symbolize a "common union" of the body of Christ, spirit, mind, and structure, and we do not yet experience *full* unity, then the integrity of the symbol is jeopardized by premature intercommunion. The pain of separation symbolizes our separation of doctrine, church, government, and so on. The pain of separation just might serve to stimulate us to work all the harder for the unity we all so ardently desire.

4. *Signs and Wonders*: The early church community was highly charismatic. But the charismatic dimension was

balanced by the guidance and teaching provided by the apostles, the participation in liturgical prayer and sacramental life, as well as the kind of social action that virtually made extreme poverty non-existent among the first Christians. From this deep wellspring of living spirituality flowed an evangelization that had integrity as well as zeal. Notice that signs and wonders "were performed by the apostles," thus inherently linking the existential working of the wind of the Spirit with the more objectively discernible leadership of the apostles. The two were not in conflict, but rather, were complementary.

The early Christian community was not limited in its charismatic expression. The Acts of the Apostles shows almost every conversion to Christ accompanied by an expression of the gift of tongues. Paul spends much of his first letter to the Corinthians teaching how the charismatic gifts should operate during public worship. It was not until the Montanist heresy of the 3rd century that the extreme abuse of the charismatic gifts forced the church to greatly limit their use in public. But even then such greats as Augustine and Chrysostom speak of great outbursts of "jubilation" in their cathedrals. The example of St. Francis and many others show clearly that the full expression of the charismatic gifts were never totally lacking in Christian history.

Today, this means that the fully integrated Christian community will have a free but orderly expression of the charismatic gifts of the Spirit. These should exist in harmony with the teaching authority of the church, not in conflict with it. Likewise, a balanced understanding of Scripture and tradition will head off the misinterpretations of well-meaning fanatics. Also, these gifts, which hopefully operate during liturgical and sacramental celebrations, should bear obvious fruit in the kind of social action which lovingly cares for God's poor.

All of this gives balance and credibility to the whole

community before a watching world as it seeks to bring the good news of Jesus to the nations.

5. *Common Life*: The early church in Jerusalem was clearly a community. Christians drew together for mutual support, fellowship, worship, and outreach. Because they met one another's needs, there were no poor among them. They were the talk of the town! Their communal life became a beacon to those around them. The success of their community values created a credibility which enhanced their evangelization. The obvious love they held for one another in accordance with Christ's teaching concerning love for the poor, was the evidence of Christ's presence in their midst, witnessing to their true conversion. Community is the testing ground for this mandate of Christian love and, I might add, the proving ground for these six building blocks. Because their lives had credibility, their words were filled with spiritual power.

6. *Evangelization*: In Acts we find that the first Christians went to the Temple daily, meeting at Solomon's Portico. In fact, this early Christian movement was seen as a Jewish sect. In the same way that the early Christians evangelized the broader Jewish community, we as Christians are called to evangelize the church at large, that is, to bring about repentance, renewal, transformation, and deeper commitment to Christ.

Evangelization will necessarily overflow from our experience in Christian community life. We will discuss evangelization in more depth in the next chapter.

I personally am linked to various levels of Christian community life. First, because I am a Franciscan, I am linked with the worldwide Franciscan community and the authority of the Catholic church. More specifically, I am related to The Little Portion, a Franciscan prayer community where brothers and sisters live out their Christian faith and where secular Franciscan Associates "plug in" through a national correspondence network. On another level, I am linked with Franciscan Mercy Corps which has a program of prayer, study, and service which we will discuss below. Finally, I am linked with charismatic covenant communities around the world through our shared Christian experience, commitment, and goals.

I sometimes compare Christian community to an oasis in the desert. The desert, or the world, is where we must be to take water to those in need of Christ's love. But if we wander too far out into the desert, we will use up our water. Consequently we will be of little help to others, and we may not survive ourselves. This is why the oasis, or the Christian community, is so very important. You must continue to be in proximity with this life-giving "island" in the midst of a burning, dry desert. In this way we will maintain the strength to live in union with Christ and our brothers and sisters. We will also be empowered to take forth the cup of cold water to a parched and thirsty world.

As Bernard of Clairvaux says, "There are at the present day many canals in the church, but few pools: of such a type is the charity of those from whom the heavenly streams flow to us, which they would pour out, for they are themselves filled. They are more ready to speak than to listen, quick to teach what they have not learned, eager to conduct others before they can govern themselves." No doubt, this principle applies not only to the "pool" of personal prayer, but of the base and foundation of community life itself, from which one can more safely evangelize others.

Franciscan Mercy Corps (FMC) is an interesting case in point. A few years ago, I began working with Mercy Corps International, an ecumenical Christian relief and development agency, to help raise funds to assist the world's poor. Dan O'Neill, chairman of the board of Mercy Corps International, and I subsequently formed Franciscan Mercy Corps, a program of Mercy Corps International. We were committed to the idea that the principles of Christian community can work through cell groups and networking in a way which will enhance our own Christian commitment, stimulate renewal within the church, and reach out to the world's poor in Christ's name. Thus far the experiment has proven quite successful and cell groups are now coming together across the country. Members of FMC may be Catholic or Protestant. They pledge to dedicate themselves to prayer, study, and service—ingredients we find in the Acts account of early Christian community.

Prayer: Prayer is the strength of our individual and community existence. It is through prayer that we find the heart of our love relationship with Jesus as individuals, and it is through the love relationship of Jesus working in individual lives that communities prosper in peace and unity. It is in the solitude of prayer that we find our true Companion, and thus learn to be better companions to others. It is in the inner silence of prayer that we hear the living word of God, and thus learn to speak words that flow from the love of God to one another.

Study: Because each FMC member is concerned primarily with a relationship to Jesus, our studies should include a balanced understanding of Scripture and prayer. Because both Scripture and prayer have come to us through the church, a working knowledge of basic church history is advised. This study of church history includes an emphasis on the charismatic and contemplative prayer traditions of the church, with a special emphasis on the rich Franciscan heritage. We also seek to familiarize ourselves with the various communal expressions of the church and to apply them to our own circumstances.

In light of our emphasis on relief and development, we commit to study Scripture, Catholic church documents, and Franciscan sources that deal with the poor and with social justice. It is through study that we discover the mind of Christ. It is through reading and study that Jesus tells us many objective truths about his being and his kingdom.

Study is nourishment for our prayer life, and prayer leads us to Jesus, the Bread of Life. Studying Jesus is like a stage of discussion between two lovers who desire to grow very close. Getting to know one another through words is a necessary and natural stage before one can enter into a stage of unspoken communication that is based on knowledge, love, and trust. The unspoken stage of communication with Jesus can only be reached after having first entered into the spoken stage. The contemplative seeks to know the truth that brings freedom to the world. The ever-growing contemplative will find a place for study.

Service: After prayer and study, FMC members seek to serve the poor. Members must always return to prayer and study to keep service from becoming dry and obligatory. A healthy life of service to the poor flows naturally from study and prayer. Our ministry flows from our being; our being is not centered on our ministry. The most basic mandate of FMC members is to live the gospel with a humble and joyful heart. In this sense our apostolate includes both our simple presence among the people and our proclamation of the gospel to the people through both word and deed. This is the ministry of "presence." Practical areas of service as an FMC member will include urging other Christians toward a more radical gospel lifestyle, simplifying our lifestyles, teaching lifestyle simplification to others, and supporting humanitarian outreaches to the poor around the world and at home.

We also encourage FMC members to follow covenant promises based on the example of The Little Portion Franciscan community:

Poverty: To live a life of simplicity so that others may come to know the richness of God's love and so that we may detach ourselves from the materialism of the world.

Chastity: To live a life of virtue, purity and chastity in our intentions and relationships with others.

Obedience: To live a life of service to the Lord so that others may come to know the freedom of being co-heirs to his Kingdom.

Silence: To live a life of regular quiet times, speaking less and listening more so that we may hear the Master's voice and be better prepared to hear and respond to the cries of the poor.

Prayer: To live a life of contemplative and intercessory prayer so that others will come to know the healing love of Christ in our lives.

Penance: To live a life free of self-indulgence and to engage in times of self-denial so that others might be comforted physically and spiritually.

Membership in FMC is an outward expression of the individual's commitment to work toward overcoming the causes and the effects of poverty and injustice. Works of mercy signify spiritual growth and reflect the personal impact of the Holy Spirit's work in our lives.

The intention of Franciscan Mercy Corps as it is depicted above is to build community where we get to know Christ, then make him known to a needy world. When the above points are engaged, stability will always be the result. It is also our desire that in our highly materialistic, affluent Western world, we should be channels of blessing to the poor in an ongoing flow which sheds light and gives life to the poor, with whom Christ especially identifies.

Whether or not we are members of such groups as Franciscan Mercy Corps, basic communities, charismatic prayer communities, Bible study groups, or other corporate expressions of Christian faith, we will have to understand and utilize discipline as individuals.

Discipline Power

There is nothing more important in maintaining spiritual equilibrium, staying power, then exercising consistent, daily personal disciplines. Frequently this will involve some kind of self-denial or appropriate asceticism, which will ultimately result in spiritual fulfillment. One of the great lessons we as human beings must learn is the priority of long-term spiritual fulfillment over short-term temporal gratification.

The discipline of *prayer* is among the most important. In prayer we seek to commune with Christ, drawing closer to him. Each expression of Christianity, whether Orthodox, Catholic, or Protestant, seems to have a specific kind of prayer emphasis which is valuable and empowering. The Quakers, for example, use a form of prayer for "centering" on Christ, in the Spirit. The Methodists use their own "methods" of prayer which relate to their central themes of "the witness of the Spirit," conversion, and holiness. Many charismatic and Pentecostal denominations pray with an emotional passion which energizes and uplifts their personal and corporate prayer lives. Catholics, with a very long tradition behind them, have engaged in various levels of prayer including liturgical prayer and devotional prayers. The Jesus Prayer, for example, dates back to the 5th century. Christians would pray, "Lord Jesus Christ, Son of God, have mercy on me a sinner." This prayer was said constantly in a cycle of repetition which allowed the person to quite literally pray without ceasing with each breath. There are those who have attributed great spiritual growth to this simple devotional prayer. Catholics also pray the Stations of the Cross whereby the final stages of Christ's crucifixion are recalled with a sense of tragedy yet victory in the cross. The Rosary, widely known but not as well understood, is an ancient Catholic prayer tradition which includes classic prayers such as "The Lord's Prayer," the "Glory Be," and cycles of meditation on the mysteries of

Christ's life: The Joyful Mysteries; The Sorrowful Mysteries and the Glorious Mysteries. When diligently engaged in, this prayer provides a sense of the whole gospel story of Jesus in the context of a deep devotional practice.

The discipline of *study* is also extremely important, particularly as it relates to the Scriptures and devotional reading. I have often said that the greatest of all tools to aid in the soul's illumination are the Scriptures. Franciscans regard the Scriptures as the greatest revelation of God for his church. St. Francis based his life on a literal imitation of Christ as he was depicted in the Bible. St. Bonaventure says in his work, *The Breviloquium,* that the creation and the Scriptures work together to form a kind of "Jacob's ladder" that leads us to God.

I recommend daily reading of the Scriptures, either to begin the day or to end it, in a cycle which regularly includes Old Testament readings, New Testament readings, and a Gospel passage. The more traditional churches have agreed upon the missal, a rotating daily schedule of readings which frequently relate to the seasons and the church calendar. Also, the Divine Office takes the reader through Scripture in a thematic rotation involving set times of prayer throughout every day of the year. I recommend these for both Catholics and Protestants because we find a point of unity in reading and meditating upon the same passages of sacred Scripture throughout the days and weeks of each year.

Fasting is a discipline which can reap many rewards but is often perceived as the most difficult. The flesh is weak, the spirit willing! In the Scriptures we find repeated examples of fasting and prayer used together. Fasting often preceded great spiritual breakthroughs among the men and women in biblical accounts and has been used historically in the history of the church as an act of penance, sacrifice, devotion to Christ and personal discipline. When we deprive our bodies of food we feel we are dying of hunger, but this is not true. We are simply so used to eating three meals a day in our world of luxury, that we feel we are starving if we miss a few meals. In actual fact, once your body has engaged the transition of a fast, it can feel exhilaration and reap physical rewards, such as breaking habits of sugar consumption, caffeine and other less healthy nutritional patterns. At the end of a fast you will undoubtedly find that your mind is clear, your reflexes sharp. Even so, your doctor should be consulted before launching into a serious fast in order to insure that you are exercising good stewardship over your body, the temple of the Lord.

The disciplines of meditation and contemplation are well known in the history of the church, particularly among monastic orders. As I mentioned above, Bonaventure concluded that prayer along with the created universe leads us toward God. St. Bonaventure, and many other spiritual leaders, believed that meditation on the created universe would draw us deeper into the mystery of the Creator. Thomas á Kempis says in *The Imitation of Christ,* "If your heart were right, then every created thing would be a mirror to life and a book of holy doctrine, for no creature is so small and mean that it cannot display God's goodness." Bonaventure said, "Whoever is not enlightened by such brilliance of things created must be blind; whoever is not awakened by their mighty voice must be deaf; whoever fails to praise God for all His works must be dumb; whoever fails to discover the First Principle through all these things must be a fool. Open your eyes, then, alert your spiritual ears, unseal your lips, and 'apply your heart' (Proverbs 22:17), so that in all your creatures you may see, hear, praise, love and serve, glorify and honor your God, lest the whole world rise against you."

Bonaventure also encourages us to meditate on the faculties of the human soul itself to lead us to God, for the human soul reflects the image of God, even if that image has been dulled by sin: "The preceding steps, by drawing us to God through His traces as reflected in all creatures, have led us to a point where we enter our own selves, that is, our own souls in which is reflected His very image. . . . Behold your own beauty, and understand that Beauty you must love." All human love should lead us to Divine Love, our human desire for truth, to Divine Truth, our human capacity for goodness, to Divine Goodness. Quoting Augustine, he warns, "Woe to you if you wander about His traces, if you love His signs instead of Him and seek temporal gain, never understanding the message of that blessed life which is intelligence in the cleansed soul, and of which the splendor of all creatures is but a trace and symbol." And from Hugh of St. Victor, "But beware, my soul, lest you be called adulterous instead of bride, for having valued the gifts of the Giver above the love of the Lover."

After meditating on evidence of God in creation and God's image in the various characteristics of the human soul, Bonaventure expects that we will be led to the Divine Giver himself. As he says on pure contemplation, "If this passing over is to be perfect, all intellectual operations must be given up. . . . Since nature is powerless in this regard, and effort of slight avail, little importance should be given to investigation, but much to affection; little to speech, but more to intimate joy; little to words and writings, but all to the Gift of God, the Holy Spirit; little importance should be given to creation, but all to the Creating Essence, Father, Son and Holy Spirit. . . . For instance, we say; God is not perceptible through the senses, but is above the senses; nor is He imaginable, intelligible, manifest, but is above all these concepts. . . . Let us die, then and pass over into the darkness; let us silence every care, every craving, every dream, with Christ crucified, let us pass out of this world to the Father." Here Bonaventure passes through creation and even incarnation to the height of classical Christian mysticism where one simply rests in the wonders of the transcendent and eternal God.

Now it is important to note that there is true and false contemplation. Francis of Assisi warned against false contemplatives: "There are many people who spend all their time at their prayers . . . but if anyone says as much as a word that implies a reflection on their self-esteem . . . they're immediately up in arms and annoyed. These people are not really poor in spirit." The true contemplative, he says, will remain at peace even when criticized. "They are truly peacemakers who are able to preserve their peace of mind and heart for love of our Lord Jesus Christ, despite all that they suffer in the world." Francis also said, "Blessed the religious who has no more regard for himself when people praise him and make much of him than when they despise him and say that he is ignorant. What a man is before God, that he is and no more." Francis also said, "A man . . . has the Spirit of God if his lower nature does not give way to pride when God accomplishes some good through him, and if he seems all the more worthless and inferior to others in his own eyes."

So, according to Francis, the true contemplative is one who walks in humility and who does not lose his peace when criticized. There are those who say that contemplatives, or those who engage in meditation, are really idle and that they despise the active life. Yet St. Francis, a true contemplative, hated idleness. For every real and true discipline, there will obviously be a counterfeit or, at least, a misappropriation of a true gift. It is important to remain balanced, to seek maturity and guidance from those who have mastered the disciplines and to be open to growth in our personal discipline experiences.

Thanksgiving is also a discipline which must be engaged in building a solid life in Christ. The Scriptures are very clear that we should thank God in all things, carrying an attitude of thanks even in adversity. St. Maximus encouraged thankfulness in and for trial and tribulation: "The prudent man . . . thankfully bears the misfortunes that come upon him." But we cannot thank God for difficulties and pain if we don't truly believe there is an ultimate reason for them in our lives. Remember the Scripture which says that all things work together for good to those who love God, for those called according to his purposes.

Praise is a spiritual discipline which can pack tremendous

spiritual clout. We often feel like praising God in the exhilaration of the moment, particularly when things are going right. But we are also admonished to continue to give praise to God even in the midst of our own personal tribulations. Augustine said, "Let us sing alleluia here on earth, while we still live in anxiety, so that we may sing it one day in heaven in full security ... even here amidst trials and temptations let us sing alleluia ... so, then, my brothers, let us sing now, not in order to enjoy a life of leisure, but in order to lighten our labors."

There is nothing more tragic in our Christian lives than to be empowered, emboldened, uplifted, and energized, only to fall into a spiritual slump. Indeed, the thrill may wear off, but the reality should not. We must see beyond our emotions and the circumstances of the hour to the eternal reality of Christ in our lives. This can be done through the application of the wise counsels mentioned above—not my wise counsels, but those concepts which have been handed down to us through the Scriptures and the traditions of God's people. As Christians, we inherit the wisdom of the ages in the body of Christ. We must see it as a great treasure bestowed upon us.

Now on to the real reason for the power. What does God want of his church? What is our primary task, our ultimate calling?

SEVEN

Program Power: Evangelization

S O FAR WE HAVE TALKED ABOUT powers: the powers of darkness and the power of the Holy Spirit. Becoming empowered (and staying that way) has been a central focus—but what is it all for?

As the charismatic renewal exploded on the scene among both Protestants and Catholics in the 60s and 70s, there was, among many, an infatuation with the empowerment itself. The spiritual elation felt good, and we shared this new dimension of spirituality among ourselves in prayer meetings, conferences, healing services, and special events of all kinds. But empowerment for its own sake is not what God has in mind. He is thinking of the world, the entire human race which is desperately in need of redemption through Christ's shed blood. Empowerment is not complete in the celebration of itself. There is more.

Since the very day of Pentecost, God has empowered his people for evangelism. Remember Christ's final words in the Gospel of Mark: "Go out to all the world; proclaim the Good News to all creation."

The twelve apostles and the first generations of Christians fully appreciated the teaching of this and other similar texts

101

and they developed from it a programme of action . . . to reveal Jesus Christ and his gospel to those who do not know him. The whole of the New Testament and especially the Acts of the Apostles show us that this time was ideally suited to evangelization and in a certain sense offers us a prototype for the accomplishment of this work, a work of which the whole history of the church furnishes a splendid counterpart. (EN, nos. 49-50)

This document is the most powerful I have ever read on evangelization and one which the reader should obtain. I will quote frequently from this text throughout this chapter. The Holy Spirit empowers us for the most urgent task the church has on its agenda: sharing the gospel of Jesus Christ. Again, the words of Pope Paul VI:

> The gospel message is not something which the church may undertake or neglect at her discretion; it is rather the function and duty imposed on her by Our Lord Jesus Christ so that all may believe and achieve salvation. The gospel message is, therefore, necessary; it is unique; it is irreplaceable. It does not admit of any indifference, of any accommodation to the principles of other religious beliefs or of any compromise, for it depends on the whole issue of man's salvation and in it are contained all the splendours of divine revelation. It expresses a wisdom not of this world and by virtue of its content evokes the spirit of faith—a faith which rests on the power of God. It is truth itself and it is fitting, therefore, that the herald of that truth should consecrate to its cause all his time, all his strength and, if the occasion arises, his very life . . . Evangelization is the special grace and vocation of the church. It is her essential function. The church exists to preach the gospel, that is to preach and teach the word of God so that through her the gift of grace may be given to us. (EN, nos. 5, 14)

The document above outlines certain difficulties in the evangelization process, among them the lack of fervor.

We have too many obstacles to contend with in our own times. We shall mention one which is complex and all the more serious because it arises from within: that is the apathy and especially the lack of joy and hope in many of our evangelizers. We earnestly exhort, therefore, all those who in any capacity are engaged in the work of evangelization to nourish and increase their fervour. (EN, no. 80)

It should be apparent by now that it is in the empowerment of the Holy Spirit that fervor may be injected into our evangelization efforts. We must have power, the power of the Holy Spirit, to accomplish our task. Pope Paul understood this truth and boldly proclaimed it in his writing:

There can be no evangelization without the cooperation of the Holy Spirit. He descended on Jesus of Nazareth when he was being baptized and at that moment the voice of the Father saying: "This is my beloved Son in whom I am well pleased" clearly affirmed the election of Jesus and his mission. Furthermore, Jesus being "led by the Spirit" went into the wilderness and undertook the decisive contest and the supreme test before beginning his mission. "In the power of the Spirit" he returned to Galilee to preach in his own city of Nazareth and there he applied to himself the word of Isaiah: "The Spirit of the Lord is upon me" and added: "Today this Scripture has been fulfilled." Furthermore, when he was about to send forth his disciples, breathing on them, he said: "Receive the Holy Spirit. . . ." The Holy Spirit is the soul of the church and it is by the help of the Holy Spirit that she is multiplied. It is he, as in the first days of the church, who acts through every preacher of the gospel who submits himself to his guidance. He suggests to them the right words which he alone could provide and at the same time predisposes the minds of the hearers to a full acceptance of the gospel and of the kingdom which it proclaims. The techniques of evangelization are valuable, but even though they be perfect, they cannot dispense with the secret action of the Holy Spirit. The most careful preparation by a preacher will be of no avail without him and no discourse will be capable of moving men's hearts unless it is inspired by him. Without him the most skillful plans of sociologists will prove valueless. We see the church today in an age dominated, as it were, by the Holy Spirit. The faithful are striving everywhere, not merely to know and understand him better as he is revealed in holy Scripture, but also to surrender themselves to him with joyous hearts . . . We may readily conclude that the Holy Spirit plays a primary part in the propagation of the gospel. It is he who moves the preacher to preach and prepares the souls of men to receive and understand the word of salvation. It may likewise be said that he is the end and the goal of all evangelization. It is he alone who produces that new creation, that is the new human nature towards which evangelization is striving through that unity in variety which evangelization must necessarily evoke in the Christian community. It is through the Holy Spirit that the gospel is disseminated throughout the world as it is he alone who reveals the signs of the times—that is God's—which evangelization receives and elucidates in the life of men. (EN, no. 75)

What a powerful exhortation! The central role the Holy Spirit plays in our mission to the world is quite obvious. He empowers us for primarily one reason: evangelization.

This document also gives support to, and predates, the popular concept of "power evangelism." Basically, this concept says that programs alone don't work. Many churches have tried program after program, yet none of them works. Only Jesus can save his church! Only the Holy Spirit can divinely empower our human effort.

It is much like natural childbirth techniques. You can go to class after class. You can breathe and push until you are blue in the face. But unless you are pregnant you will not have a baby! So it is with evangelization. You can try program after program. But unless you are filled with the Spirit as the bride of Christ, you will not have spiritual children. This is what evangelism is all about. If you are pregnant, you will give birth whether or not you employ childbirth techniques. But once you are pregnant, the program can be of some help.

There are those who would argue that the Christian's primary mandate is to worship God or to be involved in the "vertical relationship" with God before engaging in the "horizontal relationship" with our fellow man. The Catholic church teaches, however, that "the task of evangelizing all people constitutes the essential mission of the Church." The document we have just quoted states that "evangelization is her [the Catholic church's] deepest identity. She exists in order to evangelize."

How can this be? The answer is really quite simple. Just as Jesus revealed the Father, the body of Christ exists to reveal Christ and therefore the Father. The church, says the document,

> . . . in her turn is sent forth by Jesus himself. She remains in the world while the Lord of Glory returns to the Father. She stands out as the sign at once mysterious and clear of the new presence of Jesus, of his setting out and of his abiding. She protracts and perpetuates his presence. And it is above all his mission and his work of evangelization which the church must constantly maintain . . . The mission of evangelization is undertaken by the whole church and the work of each individual redounds to the good of all. (EN, no. 15)

The same document immediately goes on to stress that the church must begin this great mandate by being "evangelized herself." God's people must be evangelized by ongoing conversion and renewal if they are going to evangelize the world with any kind of real credibility.

Ironically, I have found that, while we cannot evangelize until we have been evangelized, sometimes the *evangelizer* is *evangelized* by *evangelizing*! Often we receive much more than we give, both with people and with God. Likewise, one of the best ways to build Christian community is to evangelize together.

But what is evangelization? The purpose of evangelization, this document teaches, must be to produce interior change. This means conversion in both the personal and collective lives of people to the point where it is "effecting and as it were upsetting through the power of the Gospel, mankind's criteria of judgment, determining values, points of interest, lines of thought, sources of inspiration and models of life, which are in contrast with the Word of God and the plan of salvation" (EN, no. 19). It simply means that conversion should be so profound that all aspects of life respond to Christ in a radical way.

The gospel must be proclaimed, first of all, by our witness. It is the witness of our lives which produce questions in the hearts of inquirers who see how we live. They will ask: Why are Christians like this? This is a very real means of proclaiming the gospel and it is a powerful and effective one. This might be said to be the initial act of evangelization.

It is like the first church in Jerusalem. Evangelization flowed forth almost naturally from the life of the balanced community. Because the life of the community was visibly credible, "Day by day the Lord added to their number those who were being saved." As the Scripture says of the effect of Peter's first discourse after the outpouring of the Spirit: "Those who accepted his message were baptized; some three thousand were added that day."

In effect we can say that Peter's proclamation was empowered by *both* the Holy Spirit and the witness of the

Christian community. As Billy Graham has often said, his preaching is only really effective when the local Christian community prepares the way by a believable witness of lifestyle.

But we also need proclamation—the spoken word. Remember, Peter said that we should always have an answer ready for those who would ask about the reason for the hope that we have. St. Paul asked, "How can they believe unless they have heard of him? And how can they hear unless there is someone to preach? And how can men preach unless they are sent?" The gospel which is proclaimed by our life's witness will ultimately be proclaimed in what we say. As the document above states: "The history of the Church, from the discourse of Peter on the morning of Pentecost onwards, has been intermingled and identified with the history of this proclamation" (EN, no. 22). This proclamation, or *kerygma*, is preaching, or teaching of the Catholic church. Evangelization cannot go forward without it.

As Vatican II says of evangelistic preaching: "The preaching of the revealed Word ought to remain the law of all evangelization." Or again, "The chief means of [missionary work] is the preaching of the gospel of Jesus Christ." And finally, "The Church . . . realizes that the words of the Savior: 'I must preach the good news of the Kingdom of God' have a direct application to herself. And with St. Paul she freely declares: 'If I preach the gospel, that gives me no cause for boasting. For necessity is laid upon me. Woe to me if I do not preach the gospel . . .'" (EN, no. 14).

In order for our mission to be successful, the message we live and preach must be received by the hearer and be accepted. Once the gospel is accepted and assimilated, evangelization may be said to be successful. There will be a visible entry of believers into the worldwide body of Christ. Once this happens, those who have evangelized will go on to evangelize others. As the document states, it is really quite "unthinkable" that someone who accepts Christ and his kingdom does so without bearing witness and proclaiming it to others.

But what is the content of evangelization? The very center must be the message that salvation is in Jesus Christ. Our faith is Christocentric.

Because Jesus is at the center and because he was raised from the dead, we follow his precedent in aspiring to eternal life. Christ therefore becomes the "sign of hope." This hope is not only personal, but also social. It involves family life, society, geopolitical realities, and the overall concerns of peace, justice, and development. Christ's message is a powerful tool of liberation. We must strive to free those on the margins of life, those enduring hunger, illness, poverty, injustice, and other cruelties. But this can only be done if we first realize that we must be set free from the curses of sin and death, which is only possible through Jesus Christ our Lord.

As the Vatican II Decree on the Apostolate of the Laity says, "For this the Church was founded: that by the spreading of the kingdom of Christ everywhere for the glory of God the Father, she might bring all men to share in Christ's saving redemption; and that through them the whole world might in actual fact be brought into relationship with Him. [The laity] exercise a genuine apostolate by their activity on behalf of penetrating and perfecting the temporal sphere of things through the spirit of the gospel. In this way, their temporal activity can openly bear witness to Christ and promote the salvation of all men." As Jesus himself says, "Your light must shine before men so that they may see goodness in your acts and give praise to your heavenly Father" (AA, no. 2).

Yet it is a defective gospel which only focuses our attention on social injustice and on removing unjust social structures. Evangelization strategies are sometimes so "anxious to see the church involved in liberation, that they would reduce her role to temporal activity. . . . They would assign her a purely anthropocentric function, would reduce the salvation of which she is the herald to material prosperity, her activity to initiatives in the political or social order. If this were to be accepted the church would be deprived of all her true significance" (EN, no. 32). This simply means that liberation theology cannot truly liberate unless Christ is at the center (EN, no. 32).

"Christ, to be sure, gave his Church no proper mission in the political, economic, or social order. The purpose which he set before her is a religious one. But out of this religious mission itself comes a function, a light and an energy which can serve to structure and consolidate the human community according to the divine law" (GS, no. 42).

Therefore, the content of our communication must always be built around Christ, who is at the very heart of the message. Without him there is no salvation, no eternity, no liberation of any kind.

There are various basic methods which can be used in evangelism. One method which is available to all Christians is simply the witness of our own lives. And of course there is preaching along with the use of the Scriptures. Another approach is the utilization of the mass media, a particularly powerful element in today's world. Personal contact is also an indispensable method of transmitting the gospel of Jesus. Each of us can, in some way, make a valuable contribution to evangelization through one or more of these channels. Within these methods are opportunities for everyone!

There are three very important elements we must keep in mind as we gear up to engage the evangelization process: an authentic life witness, love, and unity. Although it may be impossible to perfectly attain each of these in our lives individually or in our corporate life together, we must diligently strive for them in order for our gospel message to be effective in today's world.

As I touched on earlier in this chapter, to be an authentic witness our lives must demonstrate integrity. Again, a powerful quote from Pope Paul VI:

It is often said that our age is thirsting for sincerity and honesty. Young people in particular are said to have a horror of falsity and hypocrisy and to seek above all truth and clarity.... These signs of the times should convince us of the necessity for the utmost vigilance. We are continuously being questioned ... Do you believe yourselves what you are saying to us? Is your life in accord with your beliefs? Is your preaching in accord with your life? More than ever before the witness of our life has become an essential requirement if our preaching is to be fully effective. Accordingly, the development and the effectiveness of our preaching of the gospel depends in a large measure on ourselves. (EN, no. 76)

The message here is really quite obvious. We must practice what we preach or, as a street preacher friend of mine once said, "If you're going to talk the talk, you have to walk the walk."

The question of unity is probably the most troublesome of all. We know that we are members of a worldwide Christian family which has been fragmented through the centuries by conflict and division. The Second Vatican Council stated quite clearly that this division among Christians "damages the most holy cause of preaching the Gospel to all men, and it impedes many from embracing the faith." This is why we must continue to strive for unity in the essential things of our Christian faith. One of the steps on the road to unity is simply coming to revere one another as brothers and sisters in Christ, regardless of our various labels. We must continue the great work of bridge building so that the world may know Christ.

It is love which must animate our message to the world. Remember what the great missionary, Paul, wrote in his letter to the Thessalonians, "With such yearning love we chose to impart to you not only the gospel of God but our very selves, so dear had you become to us." I believe that the Holy Spirit, who empowers us for this great evangelization venture, also will fill us with the love of Christ to be shared with others.

As a Catholic I can say that we Catholics sometimes lack the excitement and zeal required to share our faith with others. But I honestly believe it has never before been so exciting to be a

Catholic and a Christian. As Catholics, we must stop being ashamed of our faith. Stop and think about it. We have so many of the answers the world is looking for. We have a great historical contemplative and mystical tradition, we have the most powerful pro-life movement on the earth, we have a long-standing commitment to peace and social justice and, not the least of these, is the fact that we have one of the world's greatest evangelists in the person of the pope. He speaks to more people in person and through the media than any leader could dare dream.

Protestants, on the other hand, have a wonderful commitment to evangelization—they clearly demonstrate excitement and determination. They have a centuries-long commitment to reading and preaching the Word of God. They have an unbroken history of holy men and women who have given their lives to spread the gospel.

Protestants and Catholics alike have Christ who is the Bread of Life. We have the gospel of Jesus Christ. We have a strong and powerful charismatic renewal. We also share the word of God, the Scriptures, in common, as well as many of the sacraments. We have a lot to learn from one another. If we were ever to join forces in preaching the Good News of Jesus, we could turn the world upside down!

There are many models of evangelization which I would like to discuss. However, I will simply relate how we, at The Little Portion, go out to minister. We go forth two by two into a particular area, going house to house. We do not carry tracts, we do not use questionnaires, we don't attempt to force anything on the listener and we're not trying to convert Protestants to Catholicism. We simply make ourselves available in what we have come to call the "ministry of presence." We knock on the door, greet the residents in a friendly way, and simply ask if they have any special prayer needs. We listen attentively to those needs and then promise to take them before the Lord as we return to the local parish. The response we have had so far has been overwhelming! When people sense your love and when they find they are actually being listened to (rare in today's world) they begin to pour out their hearts and share their innermost thoughts.

At other times our ministry of presence will take us to a prison or a hospital, where we may simply sit and hold the hand of a dying person. It is these kinds of loving, caring gestures of faith, when done in the Spirit, which can revolutionize the life of the listener and the spirit of the evangelizer as well.

There are many other programs in our churches for evangelization. We have Cursillo, Marriage Encounter, RENEW, charismatic renewal groups, Bible studies, evangelism teams, crusades—the list goes on. Any of these can be a viable means of ministering the Good News, but we must always remember that none of these programs can succeed if the people behind them are not Spirit-empowered, committed evangelizers.

The Holy Spirit is renewing the face of the earth. He is looking for those who would make themselves available to him, and he will fill us with power and the strength to accomplish the great revolution of love needed to redeem all humankind. All we must do is ask, then be obedient. As Pope Paul VI said:

> We must be possessed of the same eagerness of spirit that inspired John the Baptist, Peter and Paul, the other apostles and all the multitude of admirable evangelizers down through the ages—a spirit which neither men nor circumstances can ever extinguish. May it be a great source of joy to us who have dedicated our lives to the task. And may the world of our time which is searching, now in anguish and now in hope, receive the gospel not from evangelizers who are dejected or dispirited, not from those who are impatient or anxious; let them hear it from ministers of the gospel whose lives are aglow with fervour, from those who, having received the joy of Christ into their own hearts, are ready to risk their lives so that the Kingdom may be

proclaimed and the church established throughout the world. (EN, no. 80)

So is the paradox of this regathering, that we should end this book with a chapter on evangelization. It is this evangelization which is the reason for the very existence of the body of Christ. It is the church's greatest work. It therefore stands to reason that by all Christians joining together in this work, we will in some way achieve the regathering of God's people. In this way we co-labor to unify all the world in the redemptive work of Christ. In this way do we actually prepare ourselves and all the world for the coming of Christ the King.

The Music of
JOHN MICHAEL TALBOT
PRAISE, PRAYER and WORSHIP

The Regathering

A modern neo-classical work heralding Isaiah's call to *"regather the children of Israel..."* incorporating Impressionistic, Gregorian and minimalist music stylings.
Cass/CD

Quiet Reflections

Selected music with inspirational readings.
Cass/CD

Heart Of The Shepherd

In the rich musical tradition of John Michael Talbot, *"Heart Of The Shepherd"* reflects on pastoral teachings from the heart of Paul and other men of God who led the body of Christ in the early Christian church.
LP/Cass/CD

Troubadour Of The Great King

The same gentle spirit of honor and praise to the Lord Jesus Christ which inspired St. Francis of Assisi, has created this 800th year commemorative double album set.
LP/Cass/CD

Come To The Quiet

A prayerful and meditative work adopted from Psalms of David. Side One is designed for morning prayers while Side Two, for evening prayers.
LP/Cass/CD

The Quiet

John's instrumental debut is prayerful and peaceful music from this quiet troubadour. Guitar solos with a small ensemble make this album a truly worshipful experience.
LP/Cass/CD

This and other recorded and printed music from John Michael Talbot is available at your local Christian bookstore or church goods store on Sparrow.

Other Books of Interest
from Servant Books

Reflections on the Gospels
Volume One
by John Michael Talbot

Daily meditations on various readings from the gospels that
reveal much of what motivated John Michael Talbot to
abandon all in order to follow Christ and live a simple life,
marked by obedience, poverty, and chastity. Containing
approximately four months of daily meditations, *Reflections
on the Gospels, Volume One* speaks of our need to have
faith, to be honest about our failings, and to put everything
we have in the hands of Christ. *$5.95*

Reflections on the Gospels
Volume Two
by John Michael Talbot

This companion edition to Volume One contains approximately four additional months of daily meditations on
various readings from the gospels. Talbot continues to call all
Christians to live radically for Christ. His concise, to-the-
point reflections will challenge Christians to examine the
depth and quality of their response to that gospel call. *$5.95*

Available at your Christian bookstore or from:
**Servant Publications • Dept. 209 • P.O. Box 7455
Ann Arbor, Michigan 48107**
Please include payment plus $.75 per book
for postage and handling.
*Send for our FREE catalog of Christian
books, music, and cassettes.*